THE
RISE, DECLINE & FALL
OF THE
ROMAN RELIGION

PER·ARDUA·AD·A

BY
JAMES BALLANTYNE HANNAY

Privately printed for
The Religious Evolution Research Society
6 Hammersmith Broadway
London W.6.

———

1925

PORTRAIT OF THE AUTHOR AT THREE SCORE YEARS AND TEN
1st January, 1855—1st January, 1925
JAMES BALLANTYNE HANNAY

PREFACE

In my earlier books on *Christianity* and on *Sex Symbolism in Religion* I have detailed a great mass of intimate information about religions, their ideas, practices, structures, and literature, which lead up to the facts and conclusions I am now describing, and anyone interested will find copies of my earlier works in the British Museum Library and in the Municipal and University Libraries in Britain, to which I contributed free copies to let my researches be known. The great Oxford work, the *Encyclopedia Biblica*, will corroborate most of my discoveries, if properly searched. For instance, names are not always found under their initial letter, but mostly under the inclusive heading " Name." Besides, all sorts of scholars contributed to this fine work ; some are conservative and give old-fashioned or orthodox views, but, I must say, most of them have quite modern and even advanced information, but clerics cannot be expected to write with the same freedom as a layman like myself. Recent discoveries in Palestine have thrown much light on its true history and I have availed myself of this late information.

The Bible was founded entirely on symbolic names and letters, double-sexed constructions of letters or designs to represent the creative gods worshipped all over Asia, Africa, Tropical America and Europe ; and by words invented by the Romans or adopted from older religions. The *Encyc. Bib.* says, col. 3272, " Each of the many names of persons in the

v

Bible must, of course, have had some special meaning," but, (col. 3274), " Its meaning is often unintelligible."

But the Old Testament was supposed to be a product of the Hebrew priests' intercourse with an immortal god, written in an archaic script from Arab roots, which they named " Hebrew " or " Ibrim," names unknown till the Romans coined them for their new religion.

[The New Testament was supposed to be a further revelation of the god's purpose, to carry out which he descended to earth and produced a son or saviour, a common story of all nations' gods. This was written in Greek.

Thus by the use of two languages, one of which was specially invented by these Romans, and never spoken, they warded off the suspicion that they were creating these " holy " books for the purely secular purpose of governing their conquered peoples through Roman priests, by the commands of a god of their own creation.

But as the religion was to be used for ruling tribes and nations from Rome, the Romans did not call their religion the " Hebrew " or " Greek " religion, but they called it the " Roman Universal Religion," using a compound word " Catholic "—" kata " and " holos," " entire " and " whole " or " complete " religion, communicated to the Hebrews for universal or world-wide adoption.

But they took care that no " Hebrews," or " Jews " as we erroneously call them, had any part in the teaching or administration of this religion, by appointing every official direct from Rome, or at one time from Constantinople, a city dedicated to the name of the Emperor Constantine.

We shall see later how the dissyllables " opal " and " ople " came into town names.

The name Jew should be written IU, pronounced " yew," as in all old continental languages ; the name indicating double sex or a god. All J's in our Bible should be written I or Y and pronounced as our double " e," as it is in nearly all European countries, except in Britain or in English-speaking countries.

In the present volume I continue my work in showing that the whole Bible—Old Testament and New—is not in any way a divine revelation to man of an immortal god's will, nor is it true in its historical or any other statements.

It was a purely political engine, devised to enslave the people by the priesthood, under Roman rule. It is an absolutely artificial production from beginning to end, as has been abundantly proved by the researches of a courageous band of Oxford University " Divines," with some extraneous scholars' aid ; and, by these studies, coupled with my own researches, the Bible is shown to be no more authentic than Bunyan's *Pilgrim's Progress* or *Gulliver's Travels*, but much more brutal than either. It is a purely phallic creation, founded on the facts of the endless succession of life through the agency of the sex organs as I have abundantly proved in my *Sex Symbolism in Religion* and my *Christianity*.

The present volume completes my task and sums up and completes my life's work, and is quite full as a complete study of the whole subject, independent of my former works.

I have studied in many different countries when engaged in erecting plant for my many chemical and metallurgical inventions, having, of course, much

spare time during the usual delays in all new constructions, giving me time to continue my studies
and to collect information about local religious
customs and to earn the wherewithal to publish my
various volumes.

But the most pleasant and really useful time I
spent in this work was while writing my *Christianity*
and residing in a rectory—Greenford Rectory, near
Harrow—where the fine garden, absolute quiet,
and beautiful surrounding country made time
and study pass like a dream, and I was always in
touch with my "Mecca," the British Museum
Library.

Of course, the quiet of my Scottish home, "far
from the madding crowd," gave me the absolute
detachment, like Gibbon in Italy, so useful in framing
and realising a world-wide problem, which, owing to
its phallic nature prevented me from discussing
with friends. My one object in studying and
publishing the work was to satisfy my own conscience
that I was discovering the truth. I felt, however,
that, great as has been the effect of Colenso's work,
and greater still his heroic courage in defying the
(then) great Church of England—a magnificent
impetus to other investigators—yet he had not
touched on the true core of the Roman Religion
founded on the Roman-created Bible, nor discovered
the true sources of their god-names nor of the
incomes of their priests, and Colenso left the New
Testament severely alone.

For long I studied alone, and became almost
alarmed at what I had discovered, and for years no
publisher would risk touching my work; even the
Rationalistic Press held up its senile hands in horror
at the idea of publishing the truth.

But the Oxford Divines were bolder, and told the truth.

When the *Encyclopedia Biblica* appeared, a new era of hope dawned for the serious scholar, and I have taken advantage of the roads now shown to be open by this great Encyclopedia, and, having explored and mapped out the hitherto forbidden land, I have now returned to place my notes at the disposal of the reading public.

The Romans hoped to attain universal dominion through the rule of the priest and his sacred prostitutes ; and their scholars created the greatest set of pornographic books ever penned, as was inevitable from the state of their Church in Rome, whose income was entirely dependent on letting out " nuns " for sexual use ; in plain language, sacred brothel-keeping, *and worse*, as my notes will prove, and as stated by the Oxford *Encyc. Bib.* The O.T. accurately describes this reign of pornocracy, and all historians state that it was continued in the Christian era till a late date.

NOTE ON BIBLICAL CRITICISM

BIBLE criticism may be said to have begun with a French physician of Montpellier, Jean Astruc, in his attempt to trace the true sources, out of which Moses was supposed to have composed the Book of Genesis.

Many laborious scholars have since then taken up the subject, but they mostly took for granted that the Bible was really a very ancient book, and that its stories were on the whole quite authentic (Solomon with his thousand million pounds' worth of gold and silver in his temple, and all the Bible miracles included); in fact, that the Bible was a sort of "Domesday Book" of Palestine with, of course, the usual stories of "gods and men" in all ancient histories (in Greece beautifully told), or familiar tales of great men, like the fable of our King Alfred and the cakes.

But the injunction, "search the Scriptures," was first seriously taken to heart by a Scottish Roman-Catholic priest Alexander Geddes, of Glasgow, who produced by his own researches, and published in 1792, a new translation of the Mosaic Scriptures, and made the first practical, though by no means profound criticism of the composition of the Pentateuch, having no such stupendous book of studies as the enlightening *Encyclopedia Biblica* to aid him. We remember another Scottish Geddes (a lady, Jenny by name) making a practical protest against "false doctrine " by throwing a foot-stool at the parson's head in Edinburgh during his " holy " discourse, thus giving a zest to serious thinking and Bible criticism in Scotland. We Scots seem to be what the Americans call " Kickers "—" true " Protestants.

Trained in a school of exact reasoning from my profession of chemist, physicist, and engineer, first as a teacher, later as a research chemist, inventor, and practical constructor of works (and *always* a Biblical student) and broadened by astronomical study, foreign travel, and intimate contact with the workmen of nearly all the European continental countries, I have followed my old Catholic predecessor and countryman, and " searched the Scriptures," making a clear and sensible translation for myself—a work of over fifty years of varied studies, which I still continue, and I found that if I made a literal translation of the Bible, the results would not have been fit for publication, so intensely sensual and brutally phallic were the tales and language of the Bible, as will be dimly seen by one or two mild examples I shall give. It would not bear literal translation for public use. Nothing else could be expected from the state of Rome, with its phallic orgies I shall describe as being the Roman's chief joy and amusement at the time they produced our Bible.

But we are no longer left without official and scholarly guidance as to the meaning of the biblical literature, as, in the *Encyc. Bib.* we have, as the product of high scholarship and great industry, a masterly analysis of the whole Bible text, which has been of immense value to me, not so much for new views or information, as I had done most of the translation for myself—with greater freedom than could be assumed by clergymen—before that great work appeared ; but it gave me courage to go on and complete my work, as I now do, as it corroborated many "dangerous" discoveries which, without the *Biblica's* encouragement, and that of many generously appreciative letters I have received, would have made me loth to publish my present volume.

The Romans were perhaps the most civilised nation in the world at that time, and yet were the most shameless in their twelve phallic orgies per year in the public places of Rome, when hundreds of sacred prostitutes, temple women, or "nuns" (temple women under the Fish Zodiacal sign) were stripped naked and publicly enjoyed by the male population in presence of the city's inhabitants, children included. *That nation's* priests *produced our Bible.*

The feasts degenerated into wild drunken orgies, as the day wore on, as is the custom with many savage tribes at the present day—examples of which I give in my text, also in my *Christianity* and my *Sex Symbolism*, but none were so thorough, so frequent, and so popular, as those in Rome. It seems strange that a nation which produced Marcus Aurelius, whose *Meditations* might form a manly, honest Bible for any nation, should have produced those priapic orgies, of a frequency and intensity unequalled amongst the most savage nations. Do not let us forget that *Rome produced our Bible.*

LIST OF ILLUSTRATIONS

Portrait of the Author ... ... *Frontispiece*

PAGE

Fig. 1 Dorset Phallic Column ... ... facing 4
" 2 Omphalé ... ... on 6
" 3 Jupiter Thundering ... ... on 13
" 4 Babylonian and Ninevite Plaque, showing Prisoners Working under the Lash ... ... facing 20
" 5 African Timgad ... ... facing 28
" 6 Susannah and the Elders ... facing 34
" 7 Deified Osiris ... ... on 49
" 8 Egyptian Ark ... ... on 51
" 9 Ankh ... ... on 51
" 10 Sarcophagus at the British Museum ... ... facing 52
" 11 Phallic Priest ... ... on 53
" 12 Jacob's Ladder to Heaven ... on 55
" 13 Dayanand ... ... on 62
" 14 Sanyasi with their Companions ... facing 62
" 15 Pharaoh's Three Phallic Names ... facing 64
" 16 Egyptian Hierographics ... ... on 64
" 17 Nanda's Bull ... ... on 66
" 18 Serpent Lingam-Yoni ... ... on 66
" 19 Lingam-Yoni Altar ... ... on 67
" 20 Christian Cross on a Pagan Phallus on 71
" 21 Alsace ... ... on 72
" 22 Sardinia ... ... on 73
" 23 Ireland ... ... on 73

		PAGE
Fig. 24 Kerloaz, Brittany	on	74
„ 25 The Virgin of the Rocks	facing	76
„ 26, 27, 28, 29 Triform Phallic Symbols	on	76
„ 30 Indian Arch with Phallic Column and Cross	on	82
„ 31 Dorset Column	facing	90
„ 32 Christian Cross on Phallic Pillar	on	91
„ 33 Phallic Rock	on	92
„ 34 Mary Magdalene	facing	92
„ 35 Father Confessor Ankh	on	101
„ 36 Egyptian Version of Eve Tempting Adam	on	103
„ 37 Rubens' Magdalene	facing	102
„ 38 Egyptian Min	facing	116
„ 39 Origin of the Aleph	on	124
„ 40 Serpent Worship	facing	124
„ 40a Una on Her Lion	facing	130
„ 41 An Indian Una	on	130
„ 42 The Behemoth Creating Life ...	on	134
„ 43 The Dead Osiris	on	142
„ 44 Jakin and Boaz	on	162
„ 45 Egyptian Male and Double-Sex Pillars	on	163
„ 45a Lingam-Yoni Altar	on	182
„ 46, 47 Lingam-Yoni Altars	on	183
„ 48 Phallic Rock	on	194
„ 49 Mary Magdalene	facing	194
„ 50 Mary Magdalene	facing	198
„ 51 Mary Magdalene	facing	200
„ 52 Worship of the Pillar and Cross ...	facing	208
„ 53 Procession of the Equinoxes ...	on	210
„ 54 Minoan Serpent Priestess ...	facing	210

THE RISE, DECLINE AND FALL
OF THE ROMAN RELIGION

PART I

THE OLD PAGAN WORLD

THE imposition on the Western World of a book composed of mythical history, artificial god-names, Hindoo fables, and naturalistic superstitions founded on combinations of the names of the sex organs, as representing the eternal succession of life, and written in symbolical letters, representing gods, kings, patriarchs, and priests, said to have been communicated by a god to man, were the means by which Rome hoped to consolidate her conquests—no longer tenable by force of arms.

The story, composed at Galilee and Constantinople, was represented to be the revelation of an eternal god to an ignorant Palestinian clan, told in a newly-coined alphabet and language (as I shall prove), and which pretended to afford all mankind a means of eternal life and happiness after death, and escape from punishment for their sins.

Unable to crush the constant and often simultaneous revolts in Europe, Africa, and Asia, by military operations which were draining her resources more severely than did the original conquests, Rome reverted to the " Universal Religion " idea of Asoka, the Indian monarch of 264 B.C., and of the Ptolemies of Egypt, and began, at Alexandria, to make a collection of all religious documents, temple scriptures, etc., of Europe, Egypt, Western Asia, and India, to compile a universal religion, and so to end all the revolts, persecutions and massacres, which arose in most part from religious differences; and also to assist Rome to maintain the conquests she had made by controlling the priests of the conquered nations. Rome thus set up machinery for political control by priests.

Ptolemy Soter, a Greek rendering of the Egyptian God-title, Ptah-Mes, Soter, " son of God, the Saviour "—a title given to many monarchs and finally bestowed on the Roman pen creation, the Galilean "son of God the saviour" Jesus, or correctly "IesU"—instituted this movement; and it was actively pursued by his grandson Ptolemy III. and through a long line of monarchs, all calling themselves "Ptolemies," down to Ptolemy XIV., whose daughter was the fatally beautiful Cleopatra, the last of the line to rule Egypt. These Ptolemies were by no means blood relations of their predecessors, as Ptolemy (or Ptolemæus) was a title, not a family name. The Romans took possession of Egypt and her dependencies, including Palestine.

The Ptolemies' collection of barbaric sacred documents was accomplished and housed in the Brucium and Serapeum libraries of Alexandria. Many of these temple litanies were rude symbols painted on untanned ox hides, and others produced by equally Archaic means, such as clay tablets, wooden plaques, etc.

In 47 B.C. the Brucium library was burnt down when the Roman Cæsar set fire to the Egyptian fleet in the bay, while Julius Cæsar dallied with Cleopatra; but the Serapeum library, which probably contained the more sacred books —being called after Serapis, the Egyptian god— escaped intact.

There is no record of what became of those

B

religious books, but they were probably removed by the Romans to the shores of the Lake of Galilee or Tyberya, where the Romans established a college of learned men to study all religions. The duty of the college was to evolve a religion which—based on old and varied documents— would include names of gods, major and minor, and patriarchs, kings, etc., all conveying a double-sex, creative meaning. Thus the Romans' Bible was evolved during centuries of study by the " masoretes," expositors of the " true tradition," to compose their " ghostly parable " with names suitable to act their parts in the artificial Bible drama. The others will be found to fall in with the general statement made in the great *Encyclo-pædia Biblica* of the Oxford Professors, that " each of the many names of persons in the bible must of course have had some special meaning," (*Encyc. Biblica,* col. 3,271), that is to say, they were not the names of real persons, but fictitious names composed to tell a story, or as a " pointer " to the priest on some point of doctrine, and the *E.B.* is quite right, as we shall see. Most of the modern critics look for some superficial quality in the words used as names, and others seek some expression of divine quality, but all conclude, as does the *Encyclopædia Biblica,* that " very much

still remains obscure," and blame our " imperfect knowledge of the Hebrew language " ; and that " the names were in many instances chosen arbitrarily" (*Encyc. Bib.*, 3,272). " Chosen arbitrarily " shows that the story was artificial, not real. But these scholars missed, or rather avoided, the whole point, as a common-sense explanation of bible names, revealing their true meaning, would be fatal to their whole ecclesiastical business. The bible names were almost entirely derived from " phallic " roots, roots derived from the Hindoo " Pala " or Roman "phallus," the male sex organ (Fig. 1), and dealt with the idea of the god-like attribute of creating or renewing life by the conjunction of the two sex organs or the everlasting reproduction of life ; and, of course, our modern orthodox writers are loth to admit, or to recognise, that the writers of the bible came from nations of frankly " phallic " ideas, and that the two sexes, or sex organs, were the basis of all their ideas of " life," whether temporary or " eternal " ; and also that this principle was applied to all names and " holy " things. Pillar is Bowdlerised " Pala."

We get a very clear key to the whole method, if we consider a few typical names along with the " most holy " name IHOH, which we call

Jehovah, but to pronounce which was punished with death!! Why? Because it reduced the god to its more simple terms—letters founded on "creative" words or sex (phallic) words or letters, indicating double sex, as was the custom from time immemorial. All early races considered that, to create life, gods must possess two sexes or sex members on one individual—called Hermaphroditic [from Hermes (Mercury, the "lively" god) and Aphrodite (Venus, goddess of love, or of procreation); also called Omphale (from "Om," "womb" or "woman," and "phallus," the male sexual member, (Fig. 2)]. Omphale is here represented as a goddess in Greek legend, shown wearing Hercules' lion's skin and holding his "club," masculine emblems, making her double-sexed. The Greek legend tells us that Omphale met Hercules and he gave her his "club" and his lion's skin, making her a double-sexed god, while he put on her cloak and sat at her spinning-wheel; so both became double-sexed, or gods.

The lake on which the scriptures were created was called Tyberya or Tuberia (Tiberias in Latin), and is still called by that name by the Arabs. But the Romans re-named it, calling it Galilee, from Gallal, "the circle of the year," as they were

establishing a religion founded on Sun-God Symbolism. That this is true, is quite clear from their wide use of the number twelve, the months of the year, represented by the 12 signs of the Zodiac (see p. 210), 12 sons of Jacob, 12 tribes of Israel, the altar 12 cubits long and 12 cubits broad, 12 pillars, 12 wells (pillar and well, male and female), 12 Princes of Israel, 12 cakes, 12 Legions of Angels and 12 Apostles, the announcement in the Pauline Epistles, "God made flesh for us," repeated 12 times—all symbolical phrases. 12 is ubiquitous in Bible stories.

The duty of the College was to evolve a religion which—based on old and varied documents—would include names of gods, major and minor, and patriarchs, kings, prophets, etc., all founded on "creative" or "phallic" words, letters, or signs, indicating double sex, as was the custom in all religions from time immemorial. The ancients, as I have said, considered that, to create life, gods must possess two sexes in one individual. This culminated in the supreme effort of the Roman priests to create a universal god in the four sacred letters IHOH, or their "Holy Tetragrammaton" (holy four letters). It was said to be so holy that, to attempt to pronounce it, or to ask any questions about it was punishable with death.   We erroneously call this " Lord " or " Jehovah," the Germans call it " Herr" (Mister), and the French " Dieu " from the Latin " Deus." These erroneous translations were due to the fear that some one would find out, and give the true meaning, as I have done.

The I and O were easily recognised as the male and female sex organs, the " ring and dagger " for producing life in the Persian legend.   The two H's symbolise the indispensable adjuncts for life production, the " stones " or testicles, the aspirates or " breath-of-life " letters.

Deus or Dio or Dios, all Latin, and Theos in Greek, were originally derived from the Ti or Di of China, the father of abstract god-names. These Chinese particles come to us through Greek and Latin, as " divine," god of wine, and Theos, as in " theology," the " word of God," or " words about God," and so on.   But the rising intelligence of the people made the use of rude " phallic " symbols and names of the sex organs very inconvenient.   The people began to understand the use of " vulgar " words for their gods—names, invented by the priests or druids all over the world, to represent eternal life or the creative gods—when the names were spelt in familiar letters.

So the Roman clerics, as they could think of no other creative idea, devised a new alphabet and called it " Hebrew," in which the important letters no longer revealed their hidden " phallic," or sex-organ meaning. These letters were H, the " breath-of-life " letter, or " aspirate," I, the " pillar," invariably used as a " phallic " sign as representing the erect male organ, and O, the " almond," or the " Ring " of the Persian legend, that Yima, the " earthly Creator," was given a " Dagger " and a " Ring," IO, to produce all life. The letters U and V were used freely in place of O with the same significance, the " door of life," or the female organ. We shall find the combination IO in many names in the Bible, but erroneously rendered JO in the English translation (to hide the true meaning of the names), as in Joseph, Joshua, Jonah, etc., and it means a god in this sense—gods are creators of life, and IO stand for the male and female creative organs, I as a post or pillar [Fig. 1] representing the male, and O, U or V the woman's " fount of life," so that IO are symbolical of a creative god, having the two sexes necessary for the creation of life in one body, called a hermaphrodite.

But the existence of Eunuchs taught those early philosophers that the two " stones " were

absolutely essential to the miracle of life production, so the Romans put the two H's (breathing
letters, aspirates, or "breath-of-life" letters)
into the sacred name, thus making a "life-pro-
ducing" symbol, quite unpronounceable, but
which we nevertheless call "Jehovah," IHOH,
also written IHUH, and IHVH. [Heading, p.l.]

IHOH was said to be unpronounceable owing
to its intense "holiness," and to attempt to
pronounce it was punishable with death. We
translate the four-letter "ineffable" name by
a four-letter English word "Lord," while his
other name, used by Jesus on the cross as "Eli,"
a three-letter name, is rendered by a three-letter
word "God." This word is generally rendered
plural as Elohim, "gods," showing that the earlier
ideas were polytheistic. (El-Oh-im male—female
plural double-sexed gods.) But we still make
Elohim (Gods) into singular "God"—which is
dishonest; not only is it plural, but the El is a
male god, and the "Oh" female, and "im" is
the plural particle, so it was a band of male and
female gods exactly like the Roman heavenly
hierarchy.

The death penalty was also attached to touching
holy things, such as the Hebrew Ark of the
Tabernacle, or our Monstrance and Pyx, both

double-sexed articles, these penalties being imposed to guard against any disclosure of the phallic origin of the " sacred " things. " Phallic " means, as I have already explained, " sexual," derived from " Pala," Hindoo for the male organ, Latin " Phallus," Greek " Phallos," which, combined with the female, O, U, or V, represented the god as a life creator.

The four letters were put into Hebrew letters (read from right to left) יהוה (that is IHOH in modern orthography, from left to right), which no longer revealed their hidden meaning.

The Persian legend that Yima was given a dagger, or piercer, and ring, to produce life—the piercer being the male I, and the ring the female O, quite obvious symbols in such names as Joseph ; which, in our Hebrew Bible is IO-seph, an epitome of the " Garden of Eden " story, man and woman in presence of sexual passion, symbolised by Seph, serpent, a universal phallic symbol of the male organ all over the world. The serpent (cobra) erects itself and its bite is fatal like syphilis, and so it is a universal symbol of the phallus. The setting up of a stone as a phallus and praying to it is to be seen " every day and at every turn to-day in India "(Sir Geo. Birdwood in *Soc. of Arts Journ.*, 30th Dec., 1910). These were quite obvious

ERRATUM.

Pages 11 and 138: *for* יהוה *read* יהוה

symbols, the I being indicative of the male pillar (Jacob's stone set up on end, Gen. XXVIII, 18), man's creative organ or the Phallus, while the ring, O, was equally obvious as the symbol of the female organ—" the door of life." This illustrated Yima's symbolic action, still extant, of inserting the finger of a person being married through a ring, intimating that the purpose of marriage is the production of new life, or to " be fruitful and multiply," through the sex organs.

The Romans used O, U, and V, indifferently, as the symbol of the female organ (or door of life), and they placed the ⊔ I (pillar) with the O, thus, -IO-, or with the U, ⊎ or with the V thus, ⩔ , which is also our "Broad Arrow " or King's sacred mark on his goods, a life-creative or God mark. Truly a " God-mark," as all Kings were made gods on being anointed with " semen " holy oil, on their coronation. The Greeks formed a new letter Φ (phi) to symbolise double sex. Such symbols of sex coition constituted the Roman idea of " god-ship " or the god's power to create life, or even of " Life Eternal " ; their supreme god being IU-pater (Jupiter, as we erroneously write it) the double-sexed creative father or god. The old inscriptions are still standing amongst the ruins in Rome, where one may see U carved as

V and our germanised J produced correctly as I.
The Romans had Jupiter's creative wife, Queen of
Heaven, IVNO or IUNO, which we erroneously
write JUNO (slavishly copying Luther's German
I, which has a crook like J), pronounced Yuno or
Ee-oo-no, or "you know," and as M, and N,
indicate a female as well as O, this name portrayed

FIG. 3.   JUPITER THUNDERING.

the double-sexed mother goddess Creatrix of
life, Mother of all. M or Ma are symbols of
woman, because when a baby cries for milk it
begins the voice before opening the mouth, and
so calls "Ma."   As M and N are both produced
by nasal breathing, the N is as indicative of the
female as is the M.   Hence Juno is 3 times female,

U and N and O, the last being the universal symbol of the *membrum femininum*. " Una " is also triple female. But the Romans thought all these symbols too obviously capable of " giving away " the true meaning of their god-names, if they were used in composing their catholic or universal religion, so they astutely composed a new alphabet and a new language, founded on Arabic roots or Chaldean stem-words, and they also substituted, for the " ring " or " almond " shaped letters O, U and V, one symbol or letter for all three, thus *admitting that all three had the same symbolic meaning*. They made these letters as unlike O as possible, making them all a staff with a little handle top ⎤, and putting a dot above, for O, thus, ⎤⸴ and at the middle for U thus, ⸴⎤, while the sⁱmple crook ⎤ stood for V. But O or U could be indicated by a mere dot placed at the proper position by the side of, or above, any other letters, so the disguise was complete.

As to the Pillar letter I, they thoroughly disguised it by substituting a small comma written high, level with the top of the other letters.

Having completely wiped out the old phallic writing of their holy names, the Romans proceeded to create double-sexed gods, patriarchs, Priests, Kings, and men, to their hearts' content, writing phallic Bible stories, most of them very immoral, with the writers' tongues in their cheeks. What else could we expect when their occupation was letting out of sacred Nuns for prostitution—in short, sacred brothel keeping, and holding, in Rome, the twelve priapic orgies in the public streets per year, to advertise their " goods " in the open streets? It is not so long ago (perhaps it still exists), when in Java the prostitutes (Europeans) displayed themselves nude, seated in chairs in the brothel windows, so that choice could be made.

There are the usual miraculous stories of the Bible, of its being composed by so many men in so many days by commands from heaven, but we may waive all that nonsense. This Hebrew language was supposed to have been spoken in Palestine, but there is not one word nor even one letter of " Hebrew " in all Palestine, either on stone, leather, clay, or papyrus, and Palestine has been minutely searched by hosts of biblical scholars and travellers.

There have been found, however, in Palestine, writings in cuneiform (Babylonian Ninevite or clay tablets), and recently, the ruins of great Egyptian buildings, palaces and barracks for soldiers with Egyptian writing (hieroglyphics) right up to the extreme north of Palestine at Beisan, the gateway from Palestine to Tyre, the nearest commercial port.

These ruins contain large clear monumental inscriptions of Seti I. and Rameses II. The inscriptions relate to military dispositions of Egyptian troops and refer to neighbouring Egyptian cities on both sides of the Jordan.

There was no land called Palestine, until the Romans coined the name, when they were creating a Phallic or Pallic religion and language, supposed to be spoken in this land of mystery, and they proceeded to apply the name to a district belonging to Egypt at the eastern end of the Mediterranean. They also created " Philistia " and the Philistines —names derived from an identical source, Pala, the Hindoo for the male organ in the case of Palestine; and from the Greek rendering or rather corruption of " phil " (love), corrupted from Pala or Phala, they formed Philistia and the Philistines ; neither of which names were known to old historians or travellers. *They were Roman creations.* The Romans acquired this land on their conquest of Egypt, and they staged their supernatural dramas of Jehovah (IHOH) and Jesus (IesU) in their newly-acquired " no-man's-land," which had no educated inhabitants. I repeat that there was no land called "Palestine" till the Romans coined the name, "the land of the Pala" (the Hindee for the male organ), and applied to a district to which they fell heir on their conquest of Egypt, and where the Egyptian governors had fine palaces and substantial barracks for their occupying army, the ruins of which have been recently laid bare by a fine band of explorers from the University of Philadelphia.

Instead of Hebrew they have found Egyptian inscriptions and sculpture, but not one letter of Hebrew. The Romans also set up another phantom nation, to be a thorn in the side of the "Hebrews" and called it by an identical name, but derived from the Greek form of "Pala," Philis (the same word as the "philis" in syphilis, the "with love" disease), and thus invented or created two tribes of identical name-origin, the Palestinians (or Hebrews) and the Philistines, in this land of mirage. (Note that these names come from India, the "Mother of Religions.") But these Masoretic scholars gave the supposed Hebrews a holy name founded on Roman letters IU, symbols of the two sex organs (part of their ancient god Jupiter, correctly IUpiter) and symbolical of everlasting life, or the everlasting reproductio of life, by conjunction of the sexes, placed "ù

coitu," thus ⫯Ṵ , pronounced " You " (or simply
U), which   our translators dishonestly converted into a name unknown to any nation but
Britain or where English is spoken. The word
" Jew " is a fraud on our intelligence. Some suppose that, as the German I has a crook as our J,
our translators simply and ignorantly copied
Luther's crooked German I, and so changed the
name. But why did not these translators leave
the U untouched? They wrote it "ew" [Jew],
again veiling the true (if cryptic) meaning of the
symbolic IU. We speak scornfully of the crooked
and hypocritical ways of the Roman Jesuits (not
" Jesusites, " be it remarked), but our Protestant
reformers twisted the words of the Roman Bible
and called it the Word of God, thus blasphemously
calling themselves " God," as they created " pen "
names for—or disguised—the two great names of
scripture, IHOH and IesU. Our parsons all know
of this fraud, and it is becoming quite fashionable
with the young parsons to say " Yaisu " or even
Yaizu (for IesU in Latin) for the name " Jesus "
in our Bowdlerized English Bible. Blasphemy,
of course, means " speaking to the hurt " of
anyone, and the English have dethroned the
everlasting life-creator's IHOH and IesU from
their " creative god " position, and made them

into unintelligible names like those of the " beasts that perish." They have "blasphemed " the holy names. But the ancients had as their motto " God is Love," and they drew a pen-picture of what they consider " love," in the letters IU, the two " love " organs, in all holy names, whether of IUpiter, IUno, IHUH, or IesÚ, which we mis-spell and mis-pronounce as Jupiter, Juno, Jehovah, and Jesus, instead of Yupiter, Yuno, Yehovah and Yesu. The English sound of J is unknown in any other important language.

Although there is not one letter of Hebrew in all Palestine, there have been found writings or correspondence between Egypt and Babylon in cuneiform symbols on clay tablets, showing that it was a pathway for messengers passing between Egypt and Babylonia, etc., and travellers like Herodotus passed through it without finding any trace of Jews or their gods IHOH and IesÚ, as these were very late creations not yet invented by the Romans—well into our priest-fixed " Christian era " (A.D.), and unknown, I may say, " uncreated," in the time of Herodotus. They were probably evolved and applied between about .150 A.D. and 690 A.D., when the Roman pundits at Galilee and Constantinople completed their new religion, with all its documents, old and new

C

testaments and other sacred lucubrations, and launched them on the world, creating the "dark ages." In all my fifty years of omnivorous reading I have not found a single historical reference to Solomon, nor of his temple, (nor indeed of any Jewish Bible character) in stone inscriptions, clay tablets, leather or papyrus, nor of the Hebrew Kings, nor of their countries, Palestine or Philistia. The Hebrew kingdom with Solomon and his thousands of *tons* of gold and silver, were purely a pen creation of the priestly romancists. All praise to the brave Colenso, who exposed all this fraud, and was persecuted by the Church in civil courts up to the House of Lords, in an attempt to ruin him and to suppress his discoveries, but he marshalled his facts in such a masterly form that even a "Bishop-ruled" House of Lords had to bow to the inevitable, and accept his statements as the truth. He well deserves the position of our ecclesiastical Saint George of Biblical criticism, who slew the evil and poisonous dragon of the Jesuitical control of man's beliefs, which was distorting history, and strangling all our mental freedom ! The end—priestly control— did not justify the means.

Palestine was always held by Egypt, with perhaps short occupations by Babylonians or

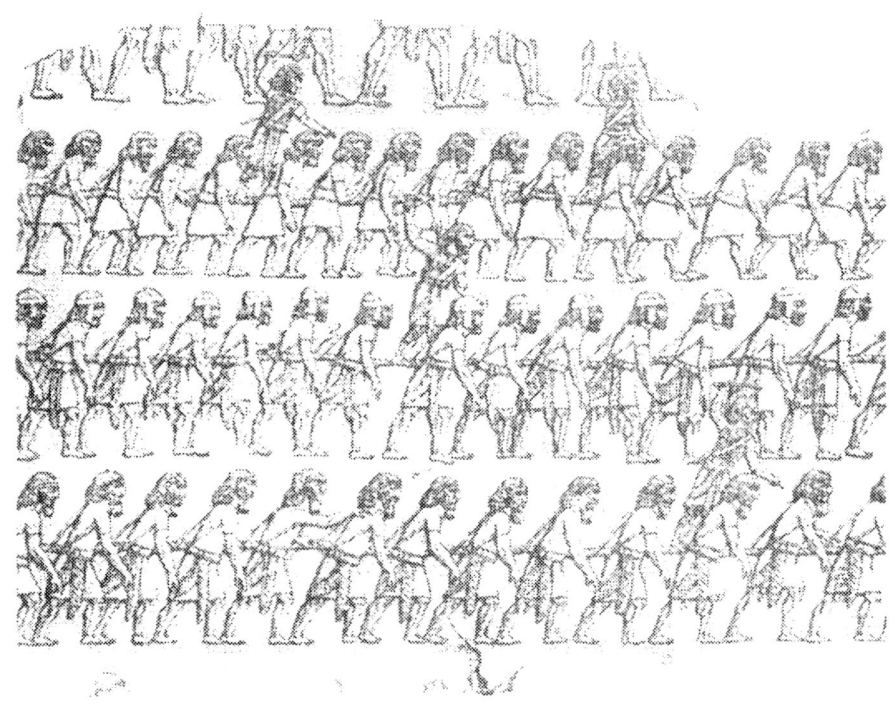

FIG. 1. BABYLONIAN AND NINEVITE PLAQUE SHOWING PRISONERS
WORKING UNDER THE LASH

Assyrians, and finally by Romans who did not need to conquer it, as they inherited it from their conquest of Egypt, of which it was a poor province, so, after the great Ptolemies, the Egyptian crown and all its satrapies fell into Roman possession.

The reputed Hebrews were only used as slaves, having been deported to Egypt and to Babylon or Assyria and compelled to work under the lash, as we see in the beautifully-executed wall paintings and " bas-reliefs " of Egypt, which decorate the tombs and temples, or in the minute and accurate portrait work shown in the fine Babylonian and Ninevite plaques at the British Museum, all showing the Hebrew and other captives working at great public constructions and the overseers applying the lash, as shown in one of their numerous plaques [Fig. 4]. Servitude was, indeed, the badge of their tribe.

The creator of the Hebrew tradition in the Bible protects himself from accusations of making fictitious pictures of the importance of the Ibräim or Hebrews by saying " the Children of Benjamin (one tribe) did *not* drive out the Jebusites that inhabited Jerusalem, but the Jebusites dwell with the Children of Benjamin in Jerusalem unto this day," (Judges I. 21) ; also " and the children of Israel (all the 12 tribes) dwelt among the

Canaanites, Hittites and Amorites, and Perizzites and Hivites and Jebusites, and they took their daughters to be their wives, and gave their daughters to their sons and served their gods" (Jud. III, 5-6)—exactly the position of the Jews or Children of Israel in Europe at this day. Where, then, is their purity of race, and where their kingdom? The idea that the Children of Israel could master the Hittites, a great nation, besides all the others, is shown by these confessions to be nonsense. They were slaves, and had no voice (as a people) in the governance of any of these countries or tribes, but were carried off to Babylon with their chiefs whenever the Babylonian monarch was in want of slave labour. But for the Romans' false history foisting their "Son of God." on the Hebrew race they would never have had a place in history nor have been heard of. This phantom race formed a convenient basis on which to build the story of Jesus. Their condition of slavery is a fine commentary on the assertions that six millions of Hebrews left Egypt *in one day*, as shown by Colenso and in my former works, and that Solomon spent on the temple (1 Chron., XXII, 14) an hundred thousand talents of gold and a thousand thousand talents of silver, that is, 5,848 *tons* of gold, worth six hundred millions of pounds sterling, and 52,232 tons of silver, about four hundred million pounds, or over a thousand million pounds altogether, quantities utterly unknown in all the histories of old nations. It brings to memory the promise to Rebekah that she was to become the " mother of thousands of millions " (Gen., XXIV, 60).

To return to Rome's inability to hold the nations she had conquered, whose revolts were draining her resources, and, by loss of provinces and incessant revolts in distant lands, weakening her more drastically than did the original conquests, the rulers decided upon the creation of a " Universal Religion," the idea of the Indian Emperor Asoka, and later of Ptolemy Soter, to be made acceptable to the various countries by including the names of the gods and holy men, prophets or seers, of the conquered countries— giving first place to the Indian and Asiatic god Kristna or Christna, our Christos or Kristos, and a new god IesU, pronounced " Yaisoo," a name constructed on old symbolism, and which we erroneously pronounce Jesus. But I and J are the same letter, the German I has a crook and is our J, and were both pronounced as our " y " in such words as yes, you, or yonder, so the name should be pronounced " Yaisoo," and is so pronounced by many of our younger so-called " high-church " clergy in England and Scotland, protesting against the old fraud.

. The name is still spelt Iesu in Germany and all southern Europe, in Italy and Spain, and pronounced correctly, " Yaisoo " or " Yaizu," the " e " being pronounced like our " Ai," or our A in " state," " rate," etc.

Further, we still put the Roman inscription I.H.S. on our tombstones for " Iesu Hominum Salvator," " Jesus of men the saviour," so the English form Jesus is wrong. All the J's in the Bible are wrong, and this may have arisen from our slavishly copying Luther's German Bible, where, of course, all I's are J, as the German I has a crook, making it our " J " and disguising the symbolical element in many names, or it may have been a deliberate fraud. The Romans even created a new hybrid language, as well as the new alphabet, and although it was founded on Arabic roots, it set up such a theoretical and complicated grammar that it is quite untranslatable with accuracy as to shades of meaning, and was certainly never spoken. The Church of England *Encyc. Bib.* says it was " unvocalised " (col. 3,272), that is, " not spoken," and " could not be pronounced nor spoken."

What language did the supposed Jews, such as Abraham, Joshua or Jesus, speak? I hold that the language, the people, and the names of the countries, are all mythical creations of the Romans, when composing the Bible, to control the nations they had conquered. The *Encyc. Bib.* authorities say that Hebrew was merely a sequence of symbolical letters, as were the Hebrew gods. If there was no Hebrew language in a speakable form, then there was no Hebrew nation. Hebrew was unspeakable, as it so involved the verbs with the purposes they were intended to express and with their relations to other words in the sentences, that each verb requires over 800 inflexions and complicated modifications of moods and tenses, with prefixes and affixes, and also in the verb's relations with nouns, pronouns, adjectives, adverbs, contiguous words, etc., to express what we express quite simply. Note that our greatest authority, *Encyc. Bib.*, tells us that Hebrew "could not be spoken," and was a collection of symbolical letters. The writers, therefore, know that it represented a phantom race dishonestly palmed upon Europe. Our own "Divines" are as Jesuitical as the Jesuits, when the writer says (col. 2,054) : "Nöldeke followed Colenso with clearer insight "and determined the value and character of the

" priestly narrative by tracing *all through it* an " artificial construction and a fictitious character." If the whole thing is admitted to be " fictitious " there need be nothing more to be said, but they uphold it still as the " Word of God." Besides, this, the Roman scholars produced *only* sufficient words to serve the purpose of religious literature, and the invention is so meagre that it could not express all the actions or things which must be clearly expressed by a living practical language.

The language sprang from theoretical rules, and never grew from infancy to maturity as natural languages do. " Hebrew was impossible as a living speech used daily " (*Encyc. Bib.*). Hebrew was " never spoken," and so complicated is it that " passages may be translated in many ways," says the *Encyc. Bib.* A language, to be clear, popular, and flexible, as well as simple, expressive, and exact, must be of natural growth, and Hebrew was not of natural growth, and was never the language of daily life, but was invented for a purpose and, as the *Encyc. Bib.* says, it was " never spoken," and " could not be pronounced nor spoken." It was never the language of any tribe, and hence all the Old Testament must have been the artificial invention of those who produced it— the Romans. The New Testament was equally a fraud, but more easy of execution, being written in Greek, a natural language. The *Encyc. Bib.* is quite right as to its artificial source, and so complicated and indefinite is it, that passages may be translated in many ways. For instance, the *Encyc. Bib.* says that " its meaning is often unintelligible " (col. 3,274). This was sometimes the translator's fault, because he refused to recognise the phallic significance of many of the phrases. The *Encyc. Bib.* says (col. 3,275): " Names were invented to fill gaps," and " the patriarchs are all mythical down to Abraham " (col. 3,274). " The fictitious character of the list [of names] plainly shows itself." " Some of the personages had no existence " (col. 3,275). " The vocalisation was chosen arbitrarily," and so on, in hundreds of " asides." [Art. " Names " *E.B.*]

One is not surprised that it took the Roman scholars over 400 years to produce a language and incidents which were " needful and apt "—if the Bible was composed on the new basis from barbaric brush writings on ox hides from all over Asia, and from " puzzling palimpsests," which, owing to scarcity of clean new parchment, the old manuscripts were rubbed or scraped over and then " covered or over-written " with new prophets' cursings or " fictitious lists of ancestors " ; " some

of these personages had no existence " (*Encyc,
Bib.*, 3,275), " Names invented," " Noah's Ark
and Tabernacle fictitious," at another place " the
equally fictitious Ark and Tabernacle," " Meaning
unintelligible," " fictitious character of list of
names plainly shows itself " (3,274), a few amongst
hundreds of the remarks freely sprinkled throughout this masterly Encyclopædia, and leaving the
" Holy Scriptures " a mass of rags and tatters.

But the writers in the *Encyc. Bib.* seldom give
explanations as to how such fictitious statements
arose. My present volume will make these points
clear. In future pages we will unravel all those
artificial names, meanwhile we will trace out the
course which Rome took to impose her will on
the countries she had conquered. She succeeded
in Europe where her troops were near at hand,
and the gentle persuasion of promiscuous slaughter,
the rack, and burning alive were freely used, but,
after struggles of centuries, she entirely failed to
proselytise her Asiatic conquests, and even her
hard-won African Empire was soon overwhelmed
by the native tribes, and magnificent cities, like
" pillared Timgad, in the Berber country in North
Africa, left a howling waste," after a very short
existence. Her whole empire, owing to its
tremendous extent and bad roads, threatened to

FIG. 5. AFRICAN TIMGAD

[face p. 28

go to pieces, and no possible military power at Rome's disposal could save it. They destroyed their magnificent African Timgad, although close to Rome, to prevent the enemy using it. It was the custom of all conquerors to destroy all the beautiful work of the conquered, to humiliate them. Rome itself suffered from the customs she had so often practised on others. Timgad was destroyed by the Romans themselves to prevent their enemies from claiming the glory of destroying it. What a fall was there from their early conquering days ! Rome's scheme for governing through religion was very simple. The dignitaries of the Church, Cardinals, Archbishops, Bishops, Nuncios, etc., being representatives of the god, held supreme power as to the anointing, crowning and deposition of kings, and this power was delegated to them by the supreme father, "Papa," or "Pope," at Rome, and Rome's curse or ban was a very "real" thing, as anyone disobeying Rome's mandate was declared an outcast, or "ex-communicated"—with whom no one dare speak, hold converse, or deal, in any way, so that death by starvation was his doom, unless he made his submission, and paid any penalty Rome might impose.

Rome's troubles had generally been caused by

the rebellion of the conquered kings or their subjects, when Rome had other rebellions, insurrections, or incursions of outlanders to quell. The smaller countries were of easy conquest, but when rebellions broke out sporadically from Scotland through Europe and Asia Minor, Africa, and Persia, right through to India, Rome found that, however easy was the conquest of these countries in detail, each individually, it was impossible to hold them all at once, if a spirit of discontent spread with the knowledge that Rome had suffered some back-set, and needed all her troops in some distant place. So it was found to be more important to have someone with authority from Rome and with a power above kings [*Ego et meus Rex*], and this was the position of the Pope at Rome, the supreme Papa or Holy Father, with his Bishops and Archbishops at each court, who could put terrible curses upon anyone defying Rome's authority. The solemn curse and excommunication by the Holy Church was much more terrible than threat of war, as war was the "trade" of all men at that time. War was a great game, calling for manly courage, whereas the ghastly secret curse of the Church, with every priest silently working against one individual, created an awe-inspiring and paralysing condition which few would dare to face. Rome felt that there must be some most sacred and holy unquestionable authority binding all these officials together so that any mandate would secure immediate and unquestioned obedience, and that influence must be *universal* so that the edict of the Papa was sudden, complete and implacable. The Church saw the absolute necessity of two engines of power, a "Holy Book" or "Bible," said to have been revealed or communicated by an almighty, powerful and jealous god, by which every priest and prelate must be bound; and, secondly, the confessional where the members of a man's family would be submitted to the powerful and intimate engine of the "Questionnaire," aided by torture, again and again, till wives and children were made to say things which condemned their husbands and fathers to torture, or to a cruel death.

The Papa or Pope was declared to be the direct regent of the god on earth, and his mandate was absolute against all mankind. The first great work which faced the Romans was the preparation of a Book, "The Book" or "Bible," the only book which "counted," and to have this book unreadable except by the clergy, so that there could be no "showing-up" of any weaknesses or omissions in the text of the " Holy " Book ; and to have a formidable form of oath to be sworn on this most sacred god's book. Rome's first task, therefore, was to create a college of priests and scholars to look into all great religions and to try to " strike a mean " by producing a Bible containing a little of the tenets and names belonging to all these important religions and to have the events enacted by gods and other characters bearing the names most important in these various religions, in fact a system well described as " needful and apt " for Government.

But the ecclesiastical authorities evidently thought that it was not a good nor a safe thing to put this book into the hands of everyone, in such a state that it could be read and understood, so, as I have already said and here repeat, the Roman ecclesiastical savants turned their attention in the first place to the production of a new alphabet and the creation of a new language supposed to have been spoken and written in Palestine.

They evolved the apocryphal Hebrew nation, with its long history from the " Creation," and its immense wealth under Solomon, and, no doubt, this task, and that of creating all the prophets and their writings, occupied them for several centuries.

When completed, they finally launched the " Universal Religion of Rome," or, as they named it, the " Roman Catholic Religion " (and Bible), " Catholic " being derived from two Greek words, Kata and Holos, entire and whole, meaning "embracing all knowledge," and all peoples, or " universal," the two words giving emphasis.

The god ideas being founded on the Creative function were given names or symbols indicating the two sexes, and the sex organs or models, which had been sacred signs for thousands of years in India, Egypt, and Rome, were worshipped down to comparatively modern times, and are still worshipped openly in India and the East, to this day, and symbolically adored by Christians, as the Cross is a purely phallic sexual symbol.

The Romans adopted the phallic cult quite easily and naturally, as it was the core of most religions, and Rome was the centre of the grossest exhibitions of public pornography, practised in the name of religion, which the world has ever seen ; as will be evident from the literature, sculpture and religious practices, of the "Eternal City " [see my preface]. As these orgies of sex frenzy are never the subject of ordinary conversation, and hence are quite unknown to the ordinary reader, it will be necessary to acquaint my readers with some of the facts well known to all scholars and students of ancient customs.

In Ireland, to take a most moral land, far from Rome and not subject to much civilisation from centres of learning, there were, up till 1790, sculptures of women quite naked, exposing the " creative organ " with open legs, *forming the keystone of the church doors;* as the sight of the sex organ, or " pudendum," especially of the female, was always considered fortunate and kept off the evil eye. [See *Plate* XXIX, p. 174, Payne Knight's " Worship of Priapus."] I cannot, of course, give unaltered illustrations of this in an open book, but the student may see all these sculptures illustrated in Payne Knight's " Worship of Priapus," a rare book, but available in the British Museum Library by application of a registered reader. Such pornographic sculpture was exhibited everywhere in public Roman Sculpture. The story of Susannah and the Elders is abundantly illustrative of this, and the reader will notice that it was a very chaste good woman on whom the Elders spied while bathing, as the sight of a temple prostitute would bring no good luck. This is, of course, only a story of exposure,

not rape. The same story is told as to Diana, the chaste huntress, who is the " cold, inconstant moon." She is always well-clothed as a huntress, but naturally, when newly born, she is naked, so it is considered fortunate all over the world to see the new moon at first appearance. But she must *not* be seen through glass, as she is then veiled, one must see her with the " naked " eye. I have seen young people run out of their houses to have no glass intervening (and even take off spectacles), otherwise no good luck would ensue. I have dealt fully with this cult in my " Christianity," as well as in my volumes of " Sex Symbolism in Religion " [out of print, but available in all the National, University and the principal Municipal libraries].

The sex members also play a great part in all Bible folk lore or fables. For instance, we have in Genesis II, 5, " There was not a man to till the ground,' " but more literally, " There was no Adam to make pregnant the Adamah," or rendered into vernacular English, " there was no man to make pregnant the woman," " Adam " and " Adamah " being the Hebrew for man and woman, the particle " ah " indicating the feminine gender. Ground and woman are both " Adamah." As Adam also means a " red thing," it may be

D

translated " There was no male red thing to make pregnant the female red thing." But there was neither man nor woman yet. The Bible stories are all phallic, even when no sex philosophy is necessary. The words may also be translated to give several different meanings. For instance, when Samuel came to Bethlehem to seek for and to anoint David as a youth, he asks for the " red thing," meaning a male, and never calls him David. But the name David is from Dudi, also meaning the " red thing " or " loved thing," so Samuel was asking for a young male. I think that these brothel-keeping priests, when they had a " dry " story to tell, could not help dragging in the " red thing," or some other pornographic ideograph.

The same thing occurs between words used in India and also in England. We say of a strong young man " he is a fine lad," and in India that word " lad," or " lat " (T and D are the same letters) means the " male organ " or " phallus," as " Asoka's Lat " is a famous iron column or phallus. We remember Asoka as endeavouring to introduce, as a universal religion, the teaching of Siddartha, to unify nations and bring peace. The same word " lad " or " lat " is used as the name of the mountain in which the Ark rested after the Flood. R and L are identical in many languages; for instance, in

ancient Egypt, China, and Japan, and the sacred
mountain is called to-day by the Arabs " Allah's
Lat " (or male organ), which is the same as
" Arah's Rat," or Ararat.   So the Ark (the fertile
female) rested on Allah's Lat, and brought forth
life, an account of a sexual creation.   It was
284 days on the " waters," the period of woman's
gestation, when " life " issued from the " Ark."
In Egypt they use a word for working native men
(like our " lad "), of which we also make use—
" fellah," which we call " fellow," and it has a
slightly phallic meaning when we say a " leud
fellow," or a " gay lad."   " Fellah " is the word
" pala " of India, the male organ, but rendered
Phalla in Greece, plural Phelim (and Phelix doubly
phallic), and other variations, so that fellah and
fellow are both indications of sex, and, as we say, of
" indecent origin."   This word " Phala " or " Phara "
(for L and R are identical in Egyptian hieroglyphics) is, with the female O, Oh or On, the
name of the ancient kings of Egypt, Phara-ons
or Phara-ohs, pronounced Far-ah-oh, three
syllables, and not Fairoh, as we ignorantly pronounce it, and it is a universal Royal title, the
two sexes Phala and O or On being joined in one
name, and indicative of creative or god-power
in man.   But even now the superstition of " good

luck " attaching to the male (or female) organ is rampant. For instance, during the War the Prime Minister of Italy showed Mr. Lloyd George a model of the complete male organ hung on a bangle on his wrist, and said, " This will make us sure of winning the war," to the visible disgust of our great but somewhat puritanical Prime Minister, who had probably never even heard of " phallic " symbols before. Such " lucky emblems " or .charms are very popular in Italy, and mothers hang them on their babies' wrists at a very early age for good health and luck, as I have seen personally in· Rome and Naples. They were even sold by the Roman Catholic priests in churches as a cure for disease, and to secure the women's fertility at Isernia at the time that Sir William Hamilton, Nelson's friend, was our Ambassador at Naples in 1781. He communicated the facts and models to the president of the Royal Society.

Modesty was unknown in early times, and in Rome in the early Christian era there were numerous fête days—Liberalia, Floralia, Lupercalia Vulcanalia, Fornicalia, Bacchanalia, Dionysiaca Maternalia, Hilaria, Priapeia, Bona Dea, and Adonai, one for each month, when " all bonds were loosed," and a huge model of the male organ, the Hindoo pala, or " phallus," in Latin, was carried in a procession, which finally degenerated into extreme licentiousness—the people indulging in the most infamous vices in full daylight. At the celebration of Floralia, Cato, not at all disapproving of the licentious exhibitions, retired, so that his well-known gravity or modesty might in no wise restrain the celebrants, because the multitude showed hesitation in stripping the " nuns " or sacred prostitutes stark-naked in presence of a man so celebrated for his modesty. I can find no record of the children being kept indoors while this was going on. These " feasts " were repeated every month, while other nations had only two or three such " Holy " days, Spring and Autumn with some ; and Spring, Mid-summer and Autumn with others. But they were universal, *and are so yet, with savage nations*, as, in one sense, the Romans were. In my former work on " Christianity," I give full accounts of such celebrations all over the world up to the present day. I merely state enough here to illustrate my narrative.

I may say that in every part of the world there have been joyous festivals (feasts), carnivals (flesh-eating banquets), where, after partaking of food and drink, promiscuous sexual intercourse is indulged in. Many African tribes practise these, especially at Spring-time and at harvest, as did the Hebrews in their " sacrifice " to IHOH, also called a feast, commanded by the " Lord God of Israel " (IHOH of the Elohim)—" Let my people go, that they may hold a feast ["Hag"] to me in the wilderness " (Ex. V, 1). [I often wonder where was the shorthand reporter to " take down " verbatim all the speeches of gods and men reported in the Bible]. These feasts were called " sacrifices," but we must remember that the word " sacrifice " only means " to make holy," so that any action, " however vile," is a " sacrifice " if it is held to be holy by the priest. We know that at another " Hag " the Israelites were " made naked unto their shame " (Ex. XXXII, 25), and that was their practice, as we know such feasts are held up till this day all over the world, as many travellers have described, when " all bonds were loosed," and the " great sacrifice " was performed. This was revived in a mild form in Germany before the War under the name of " beauty evenings," the participants exhibiting the human form entirely naked—both sexes being present. The court held these " Hags " to be quite innocent, but they were stopped. (See my " Christianity," p. 226.)

That they called this " Hag " *the great* sacrifice shows how much it was enjoyed by the Hebrews. This promiscuous intercourse was also performed at the Feast of Tabernacles (see my " Sex Symbolism "), the " holiest " feast of the year, so phallism was the basis of the Hebrew religion as painted for us by the Romans. It was, however, only a picture of what the Romans themselves were doing, and is still done by all Savages such as the Uapés on the Uapé river, a tributary of the Amazon. The *Times Lit. Sup.*, Nov. 20, 1910, tells us :— " They hold feasts to Jurupari, the Chief Member of their Trinity, when the young men go through initiatory rites. The women are then invited to a " great sacrifice " which, like the Hebrew Hag, consists in a wild orgy of promiscuity and drunkenness and acts of unspeakable immodesty and frenzy when "all bonds of relationship" are "untied."

Such as these were the public celebrations of the joyous act of creation of new life, illustrating mankind sharing in the miraculous power of the creative gods, and they were approved of by the city fathers of Rome. Similar phallic processions still take place in India (see Dr. J. C. Oman's " Cults, Customs and Superstitions of India ").

These joyous outbreaks were repeated annually, monthly, or even more frequently, down to weekly or nightly, as in the " Agapæ " of the early Christians, when the " male and female saints " lay together all night in the churches to increase their " religious zeal," so that one famous Roman declared he would rather see his wife a temple prostitute than a Christian. " Religious zeal " consisted at that time in a liberal use of the temple Nuns. These were public exhibitions, whereas the steady commercial exploitation of prostitution belonged to the priesthood in the temples under dignified conditions resulting in the accumulation of great wealth in which the State shared.

One notes with astonishment that there is no mention of keeping the children indoors while such orgies were taking place. There are no such restrictions in India (as Dr. Oman tells us, when he was present at the " holi " festival) at the present day, " girls and boys listened eagerly to the licentious rhymes," and " looked on while gross acts of indecency were perpetrated." (See Dr. Oman's " Brahmins, Theists and Muslims of India," p. 247 *et seq.*). Again, in Dr. Oman's " Cults, Customs and Superstitions of India," he describes wedding songs thus :—" Songs were sung by the women of the party with the greatest gusto and enjoyment, and these songs are simply outrageous in their grossness. They are not extemporised, but are so framed that any names may be introduced into them. The singers bring in any names they please, with the result that the persons whose names are inserted find themselves accused before the world, in the most undisguised language, of having committed grossly immoral or even incestuous actions, and possibly the charges may have some truth in them. Men and women, *and even children*, listen and laugh, but no one takes offence." It saddens me to remember that Dr. Oman, a dear friend and my pupil in chemistry, has long since joined the "great majority."

We have many records which tell of a thousand prostitutes—Nuns, or Temple women—being kept at each of the temples, such as those of Corinth and Eryx, and the fame of Paphos in the island of Cyprus was such that "paphia" was synonymous with "prostitute," and Paphos and Paphia represented the male and female sex organs, as well as the male and female prostitutes maintained at the temples. In fact, prostitution by women, and in other debased forms, was a "Holy Office" at all temples in the B.C. era, and down to the time of Michael Angelo, about 1520, and indeed it seems to have improved very little in later times, because, as late as 1836, the number of births in Rome was 4,373, and of these 3,160 were illegitimate, or nearly three quarters of the children born were due to the Church's immorality.

Lecky's "History of European Morals," and the "Syrian Goddess" of Lucian, will give my readers further information, which I cannot repeat here. St. Augustine, a great Christian, ordered that the women attending religious Christian meetings should wear "clean linen," as the "Holy Kiss" (meaning promiscuous sexual intercourse) was administered—lying in the churches all night, to increase their "religious zeal"; and even the practice of "concubitus Œdipei," which was otherwise severely punished, was freely indulged in. Free prostitution, no fees, of the new Christians, enraged the old temple priests by taking away their income. Christianity was the same as paganism, *but no fees were payable*, the Christ had made the "great sacrifice" quite free; similar to what Cunningham Graham tells us of a town of Spanish South America, where it was said "all the women here are amateurs," so a brothel would yield no profit; so in old times the official Roman priests' fees dwindled owing to the "free" Christian practices. In later times, laws were passed to prohibit priests from living with their mothers or sisters, as this had always led to incest, which had been considered a terrible crime (*vide* " Œdipus Rex"), and it had been very prevalent in poor countries, where priests were not sufficiently wealthy to be able to keep a concubine. The Christian or " New " Churches were simply " free trade " brothels like the " high places " of the O.T., where, however, all prostitutes had their fees, as is shown in the story of Tamar and Judah; where she, acting the part of a professional prostitute, says, " What wilt thou give me that thou mayest come in unto me," and, like many a modern youth, he gives her his signet, bracelet, and his staff (equivalent to the modern watch and chain) to keep till he redeems them by money or its equivalent—a kid (Gen. XXXVIII, 12 *et seq.*).   We have seen an attempt to revive the " free love " religion, prostitution-without-fees system by Piggot's " Abode of Love." The prostitute often lived over the " chief gate " of the town, and was a public functionary who was the source of all " news," as in India to-day. The Emperor Titus is reported to have left valuable gifts for the benefit of the maidens, whose " converse " he had enjoyed, and for the temple treasury, when he visited Paphos on his way to subjugate Jerusalem. Every temple had numerous cubicles for the practice of religious prostitution—some had hundreds to accommodate their patrons on fête days. These little rooms of about eight feet by five feet surrounded the holy temple—built in the walls, three tiers in height, surrounding the inner sacred chamber, and said to yield in the Jerusalem temple 100 of such cubicles for sexual intercourse or the worship of Venus, called Debir by Lucian (see *Encyc. Bib.*, cols. 4,929 and 4,946, or the "Syrian Goddess" of Lucian).

These chambers were called Selaoth or Lesakoth, (both words are given in the *Encyc. Bib.* under "Temple.") Selaoth is quite clear, meaning "chambers for men and women, double-sex chambers," also for "refreshment," while Lesakoth means "for the purpose of being joined"; the same word meaning also for the "interchange of liquids," one of the very literal and rather disgusting realistic words of those ancient savage Romans in the *Encyc. Bib.* Sela is a double-sexed word used throughout the Psalms as an ejaculative, calling upon the god, equal to "Amen" —ah-min, female-male used ejaculatively for male-female god. The amen, or Ah-min, was a popular god in Egypt. Selah, Sel variant of Sur, the "Rock that begat thee," and the female particle A or Ah giving double-sex; or a god. Lesakoth is an inversion of Selaoth.

The " Hebrews " also use words beginning with " m " for " female " things, and " P," for " masculine," and we have Massekah and Pesselim, feminine and masculine words, equivalents of our mortar and pestle, and worshipped as a god like the Dorset pillar, which mean things which " pour out "—they were very literal, those Romans who created " Hebrew." Nearly all their words about sex organs have a meaning of " pouring out of liquids," which our translators render by such phrases as a " Drink offering to the Queen of Heaven," and such disguises as their ingenuity can suggest, " molten images," for instance. These words as names of idols were simply models of the sex organs, and one has to consult and examine, and in fact " analyse " all the references possible to find out the true meaning of many of the words, such as Massekah and Pesselim coupled together in the Bible. Pesel is given as a " carved image," but it is made up of the three particles, the first, P, which is always " Palic," or in the Roman form " Phallic " (" Pala " in Hindoo and " Phallus " in Latin signify the male organ), then comes Es, flesh, Hindoo for the " flesh of his nakedness," and finally El, god, so the Pesel means the male organ, worshipped as a god, like the Dorset pillar. [" Pillar " is simply the Hindoo

" Pala."] Pesel, pronounced Peezel, is used in Scotland as a name for the male organ amongst boys. Pesel is translated " that which pours out," and this is foolishly translated in our Bible as a " molten image," also a " graven image," and lastly as an " idol." In " Idol " we have a word composed of I, the pillar god, and Ol, the Phoenician form of Al, El, Il, etc., the name for god (Jacob's god), the two combined by the copulative D, sacred in China, making Idol, or " pillar god." This is also translated as that which " pours out," which cleverly describes its double functions, and this, again, is coupled with Massekah, a female noun, beginning with Nesek (observe that M and N are equivalent), which also means " coition," or " going together," or " mingling," also " to pour out," and both Pessel and Massekah mean " mingling " or " going together," " mix," " melt together." These Pesselim or phalli have been found in tens of thousands at all great shrines, carved in various common and precious stones, and in all sorts of metals. They have also been dredged up from the Tiber, the Seine, and the Thames rivers, cast in lead and bronze, so we see how ubiquitous was their worship or use as " charms," as in Italy to-day. (See Payne Knight.)

I repeat that Massekah means "mixture," which we call "coition," "going together," and Massekah and Pesselim are female and male "things" which "pour out," "mingle, and mix" —all out of *Davidson's Lexicon*, issued by Bagster. They also mean the mortar and pestle, utensils which we use for "mixing" or "mingling"; and the Bible, as translated, is full of these "side

Fig. 7.—Deified Osiris.

Lauzoni gives this piece of symbolism from Egypt. Two phalli supporting the sky over the dead Osiris, and the mortar and pestle with the two stones under the sacred Bull carrying the dead Osiris. The same symbolism as the Rod of God and two stones (of Moses) in the ark. Ark and mortar are woman.

issues" raised by the translators to bemuddle, or hide the true meaning, yet secretly capable of exposing it quite fully. Mortar and pestle are used phallically in India and Egypt as symbols

of eternal life, as in this Fig. of Osiris on the bull.
(Fig. 7). In Massekah we have a good example
of the equivalence and identity of " M " and " N "
in Hebrew composition. The root of Massekah is
Nesek, sometimes used, from its meaning (to "pour
out ") as a drink offering, probably the drinking of
wine at their great " Hags," when " all bonds were
loosed " and promiscuous sexual intercourse was
performed by the celebrants in the Court of
Women during the Feast of Tabernacles, as
described in my " Sex Symbolism," Vol. I, pp.
400–402, and more fully in Vol. II, pp. 580–582.

Nesek is given a totally different signification
from its derivative Massekah—to " bite or to
vex "—and we know that these promiscuous
phallic orgies led to great epidemics of syphilis,
as in the outbreak mentioned in Numbers XXV, 9,
when 24,000 (! ! !) Philistines died of an incurable disease through touching the Hebrew Ark
(woman). " Emerods on their secret parts " says
our Bible. But the word used, Ophelim, means
" disease of the two sex organs " (see my " Sex
Symbolism," Vol. II, p. 208; for the prevalence
of syphilis see my " Christianity," pp. 231–234.)

In this Egyptian Ark we have several phallic
symbols of eternal life from left to right, ankh,
two sexes combined, then a phallus, then the ankh

dissected into its male and female elements, emitting creative rays (centre), flanked to the right by a repetition of phallus and ankh—all signs of

FIG. 8.—EGYPTIAN ARK.

Ankh. The origin of the ankh was the combination in coition of the two sex organs producing life, as in this sketch where the "rod and almond" join up to form the ankh.

FIG. 9.—ANKH.
Origin of the ankh (handled cross),
double sex creative symbol.

E

eternal life. (Figs. 8 and 9.)   In this sarcophagus from the British Museum (Fig. 10) the three signs of eternal life are portrayed.   At the top is the ankh, the combined male and female organs, with two upraised arms, praying to "high heaven." Then we have a "Thet," the conventionalised male organ in the female, producing life; at the foot is the phallus in the vagina with the womb above, disguised by British prudish scholars as the "buckle" or "tie," when they know it is no such thing. Let us note that in all sets of burial caskets the inner most holy one seldom or never has images of gods. The recently found tomb of "Dad ankh Amen" (erroneously "Tutankamen") has outside plenty of gods, while the second has few, and the inner, "most holy casket," has only the Ankh and Thet symbols and no images of gods. The priest's terrible duties, amongst all the incurable disease, must have made him very hard-hearted and avaricious, and he praises the cheat and the cowardly robber; as witness the tale of Jacob and Esau, or, as it should be, Esu, the "aleph," or A, being silent.

The priest-written Hebrew Bible is very hard on gentle, good-natured men, and the tale of Esau and Jacob is a good example of their ideas and literary wares. Esau, really Esu, means Es,

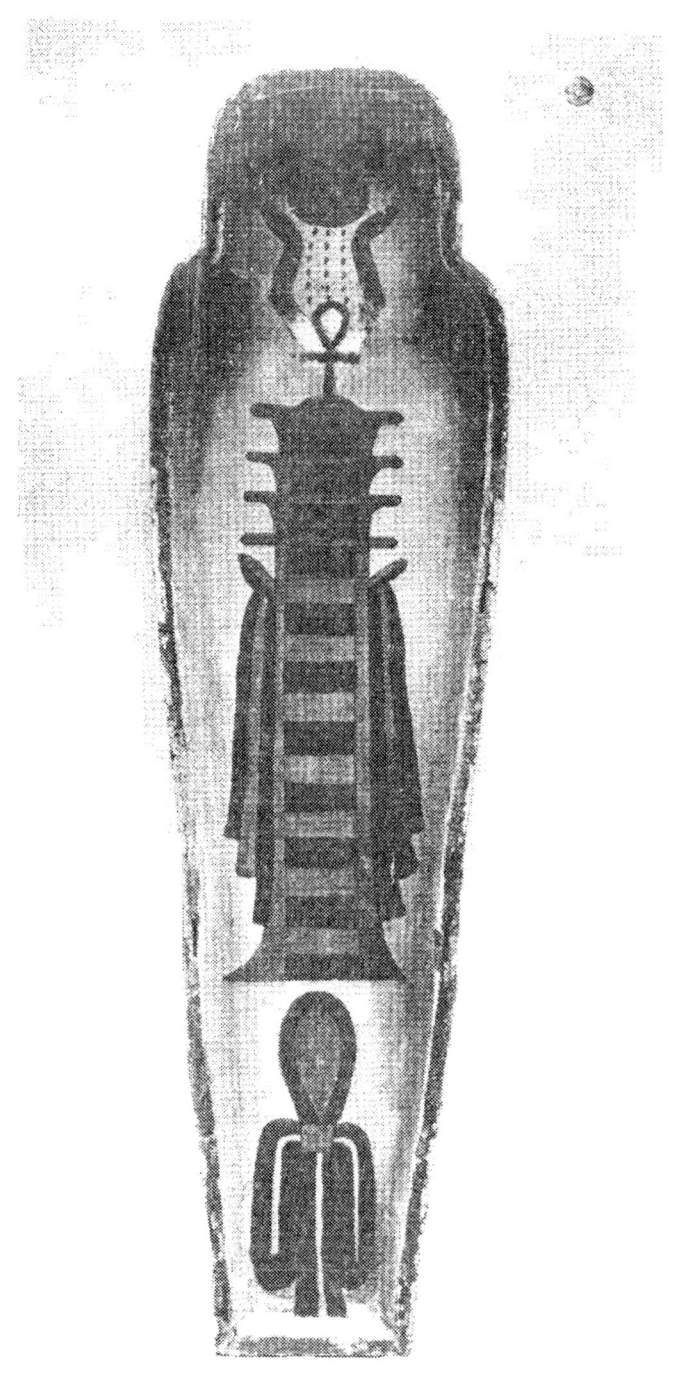

FIG. 10. SARCOPHAGUS AT THE BRITISH MUSEUM

"flesh," and U, "woman," the name meaning "flesh of woman," a very soft, kindly man, and it says he was "hairy," which does not necessarily mean hairy on the hands only, but hairy like "woman." This Es is the particle making the name of IesU, Jesus. We may note that the priests of many countries are shaved, as shown in

FIG. 11.—Phallic Priest.

Fig. 11, so that long hair was contrary to the priestly concept of strength of character.

But Esau is also called Edom, where Ed is the male "witness" or testicles, and "om" is woman, meaning that Esau, though a male, having the "witnesses," was sexually as soft or gentle as a woman, a kindly gentle soul (as he is in the text), the sort of person the priests despised, while the fluent liar Jacob gains everything. Fine morality ! ! ! Then we find in 2 Corinthians XI, 14, " Doth not even nature itself teach you that if a man have long hair, it is a shame unto him, but if a woman have long hair, it is a glory to her ? " So Esau, being a gentle soul (as the story proves) is robbed of all his rights by his dishonest brother and is condemned to be " down and out," as far as his family is concerned, owing to his gentle, woman-like disposition.

Thus the priest taught ruthlessness and low cunning as the successful traits of character.

Jacob's name in Hebrew means " to supplant," " circumvent," " defraud," " insidiator," " supplanter," " fraudulent," " deceitful," " taking by the heel "—a fine character of the favourite son, favoured also by Jehovah.

The mother sends Jacob away in fear that Esu might kill him, and on his way he dreams of a " ladder to Heaven," which is a universal phrase for a virgin, the *barred* form of the *ladder* indicating the " virgo intacta," and the idea of a fresh virgin being " Heavenly " to these brothel-haunting Hebrews is no doubt a portrait of the Roman clergy. The priest (Fig. 12) is worshipping the virgo intacta indicated by the " barred " ladder to

Heaven.   The seven-rayed star at the top means woman (Babylonian).   The *Encyc. Bib.* tells us that the holiness of Kadeshim " (male prostitutes) and Kadeshoth (female prostitutes) consisted in separation, set apart, at puberty, from the households

FIG. 12.—JACOB'S LADDER TO HEAVEN.
Virgo Intacta Worship.

in which they grew up, according to a custom still extant which ranges from the Gold Coast to Tahiti."   (Frazer's " Golden Bough," II, 225 ff.).

In column 837 of the *Encyc. Bib.* we find " The offer of the body " in *honour* of the deity (what about adultery ?) prevailed widely in Northern Semitic religions, a special class of temple harlots was maintained," " Commerce with them was a religious act," " The hire was sacred, and was bought into the treasury of the god " (simply brothel keeping). The *Encyc. Bib.* says (col. 3,615), " The places Paul visited were famous for ' filthy sensuality.' The characteristic of the worship at Paphos " [where Paul visited] " lay in the strongly organised college of priests and priestesses living in thousands round the temple, and the sexual excesses of the devotees constituted the Cyprian cultus of the deification of lust." Jerusalem was said to be more corrupt than Cyprus.

The early Christians lay in the temples all night for promiscuous sexual intercourse, and the prostitutes were " highly respected." Saint Augustine commanded ladies who attended the " Eucharist " to wear " clean linen," as the " Holy Kiss " was administered. Jesus (correctly IesU), pronounced Yaisoo or Yaizu [hard s], is made to feebly condemn ecclesiastical prostitution, by rebuking the sale of " Doves " *in* the Temple. This no doubt referred to having sexual intercourse like the early Christians in the Temple itself to escape paying fees, instead of retiring to and paying for the little chambers, " Lesakoth," of which there were hundreds at large temples (100 at Jerusalem) for the devotees "melting together" as Lucian explains. These cells were also called "debir" (*Encyc. Bib.*, col. 4,938, article " pestilence"). These cells were in mysterious gloom, exactly as described by Lucian. The priests "leaped and danced " before the Altar (as did David before the Ark) with naked " Palals," leading off the promiscuous sexual intercourse. Jesus is supposed to rebuke prostitution as sale of " doves " in the Temple, but we must remember that there were private cells, " Lesakoth," for sexual intercourse, and Jesus was rebuking the open prostitution in the Temple itself, as the Christians were latterly doing, with no fees to pay. " Dove " always indicates openly demonstrative love, as seen when doves flock together, and, when Mary anoints his " feet " and is closely associated with Jesus throughout all his life, Jesus plainly tells Martha that " Mary hath chosen the better part," " nun," or " fish " woman, the priests' concubines, also by obtaining the revenues of the Church, at that time entirely derived from prostitution, by " washing " men's " feet," a phallic phrase, and drying them with her " hair," an impossible towel ; but " hair " has also its phallic significance, th supporting the *Church*, while poor Martha only made a comfortable and happy home for some man or family, our modern idea of the "better part." Forlong gives examples of "foot" and "feet" used in a phallic sense, and we have examples in Ruth and in Deuteronomy XXXIII, 57, "the young one that cometh out from between her feet," and in 2 Sam. XIX, 24, "dressed his feet, trimmed his beard," again "feet and hair." It is a curious commentary on the voyages of St. Paul, that the towns he was said to have visited, were the most famous or the "worship of Venus," or for prostitution, or, as the reverend writers in the *Encyc. Bib.* say, for "filthy sensuality," but their own Bible seems to lead in such matters when properly translated, as I shall show.

The *Encyc. Bib.* says, "there is no epistle of Paul," in fact, that he is only a "pen-name" introduced to argue against circumcision and to eliminate circumcision from their religion. His name is that of the male organ Pala, Pall, Pul, Pawl, or Paul, in Hindee and English. The *Encyc. Bib.* denies that any Epistles were written by Paul. "There are none of them by Paul" (*Encyc. Bib.*, col. 3,625). "There is no Epistle of Paul," and the Encyclopædia writer condemns them in detail one by one, and in another (column 3,627) says that the principal Epistles " cannot be the work of Paul " (see my " Sex Symbolism," Vol. I, p. 261). All criticisms on the life and activities of Paul are of a " purely negative character " (col. 3,630, *Encyc. Bib.*), which means that no such man existed ; he is a creation of the Ecclesiastical pen, as was all our " Bible." Paul's writings were issued by the Roman Catholic Church to make a new " universal " or " Catholic " religion acceptable to all nations, circumcised or uncircumcised alike, and to make the Hindoo god Christna, and a new god they were introducing, also of Hindoo origin (IesU), our Jesus, acceptable to all countries held by Rome.

" Irrevocably passed away," are all these " ideas, theology and system of Paul, the right foundation being wanting," (*Encyc. Bib.*, col. 3,630). " They—all of them—have disappeared, they rested upon a foundation, not of rock, but of shifting sand " (*Encyc. Bib.*, col. 3,630). Paul was a mere creation of the priestly pen—as I shall prove nearly all the biblical characters to have been—merely symbolical creations. It is a curious commentary on the supposed voyages of St. Paul that the towns he is said to have visited, Antioch, Lystra, Salamis, Papho, Perga, Pisidia, Pamphilia, Iconium, Athens and Corinth, are mentioned by contemporary writers as being the most important centres of religious prostitution, and we must remember that his name, " Paul," is simply our word Pole, Pawl, Pall, etc., from Pala or Phala, the 'male organ of reproduction. [This is dealt with very fully in my "Christianity" and my "Sex Symbolism," available in all University libraries.]

Paul was introduced to argue " circumcision," or " uncircumcision," against those who, like the other pen-creation, Peter, represented the strict cult of cutting the foreskin of the male organ, which was at one time nigh universal, even in Britain, as I show, in Fig. 1, a circumcised Phallus from Dorsetshire—in fact, Paul represents the reformers who left the surgical treatment of the phallus outside the code of the new Christian religion with which the Romans were preparing to consolidate their rule.

Religious prostitution precedes the earliest dawn of history, and we find in Egypt among a list of transport tariffs between Coptos and Berenicia a charge of 108 drachmas for each slave for prostitution.

When the priests set up their imaginary gods, who were said to have miraculously created this universe " in the beginning," they naturally looked for some method of naming them, and they could find no better method than to combine the names of the two sex organs necessary to the creation of new life, a method of nomenclature which goes back to the dawn of human intelligence.

This method was also employed as their means of naming their religious paraphernalia, which might be " palaphornalia." Altars, arks, church furniture and dress, so the names were double-sexed in all countries to express the gods, goddesses, saints, apostles, kings, along with all the parapher-nalia involved in the exercise of their functions with the " Pala." It must not be forgotten that, in India, which is truly named, as my studies show, the " Mother of Religions," the bulk of the people in ancient times went entirely naked, as do their sacred men, Yogis, to this day, so there was no sense of shame connected with words or images representing sexual organs. Their Yogis, or ascetic religious teachers, still hold nudity as sacred, and teachers, such as Dayanand, whom I have met in England in frock coat and top hat, go entirely naked in India, as I show in Fig. 13. The Indian word representing the male organ was and is " Pala," which has derivatives in every country in Europe and Asia, and there was a " Pal " dynasty in India in past times. This word has become corrupted and is written Pela, Phallus, Pul, Phil, Phyl, Pole, Pel, Phulus, and so on. There were " Pal " lines of kings, such as

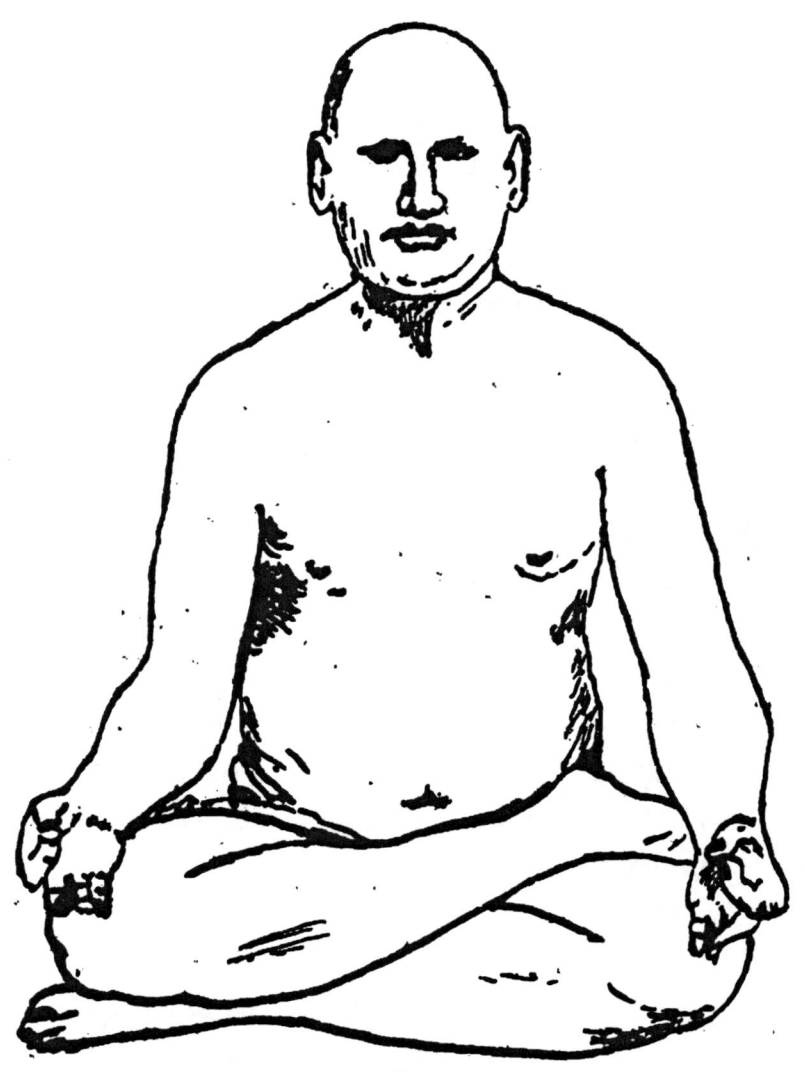

FIG. 13.—DAYANAND.

Assur-bani-pal, Assi-nazir-pal, a dynasty lasting
over several generations, and the word has sunk
into the languages of many countries. Even the
great Pharaohs of Egypt have this appellation.
Egyptian has only one sign for R and L, and
unfortunately the first readers of the hieroglyphics
chose the wrong letter, as the kingly title of
Egypt is one of these double-sex names, from the
male Pala of India coupled with the female ring
or oval O; so the name should be Phala-O, or
Phala-Oh, not Phara-oh, as we write it, and
certainly not Fair-oh, as we pronounce it. The
native ear is quite retentive, and the native speaks
of the nude, working Egyptian as a Phala or
Phellah, the terminal " a " or " ah " being in this
case the female symbol, as frequently used as the O.
Some speak of the Egyptian fellah, our word
fellow, or plural fellahim, or fellahin, " m " and
" n " being used indifferently (the eastern plural,
as in the Hebrew Bible; "Eloh," god, "Elohim,"
gods, plural). So the " Fairo," as we call the
Egyptian ruler, should be Pala-o or Phala-o,
not Phara-oh, and it is so written on the monu-
ments. In Greece "pala" became "phallos,"
and in Latin "phallus," from which we derive
the adjective " phallic," used to describe all literature, sculpture, or religious worship, faiths, or

emblems, referring to the reproductive organs as representative of creative power; and so, in ancient times, all exercise of that power, even by public prostitutes, constituted a sacred act.

I give here from a carved list of Egyptian kings one claiming in his cartouche a triple phallic power (top of middle column). It was largely used in Egyptian hieroglyphics, as instanced here; the word " poison " is rendered by a group containing the phallus, as will be found in any text book (See Budge's *First Steps in Egyptian*.)

melu

poison.

FIG. 16.

In Rome it was called the Phallus, so that Greece and Rome adopted the Indian name, P and Ph being considered identical, but added the masucline determinant of each nation. The common people in India call it " Ling " or " Lingah," or even " Lingam," but " Pala " is the religious name in India. The female organ is called, in Hindee, the " Yoni," which might be written in English orthography " ee-on-ee," both Y and I pronounced like double e, and never, as in English,

FIG 15. PHARAOH'S THREE PHALLIC NAMES

as " eye," and the On is, like Om, a world-wide symbolic term for the female. I am sorry to say that English, the richest language in the world, is the most stupid in vowel pronunciation and in its spelling, especially in foreign names. Take the name of the prophet Isaiah, which we pronounce Eye-zay-yah, when every other nation pronounces it Ees-ah-yah, or the often-mentioned Pharaoh, which we pronounce Fair-oh, while it should be Far-ah-oh, which makes a very clear, intelligible name, " Phara " or " Phala ", " oh," female [r and l are identical in the Egyptian alphabet], which should be a word of three syllables, Far-ah-oh, while we turn it into a word of two syllables, Fair-oh, and then mispronounce it. The mispronunciation has long hidden, from even intelligent people, the true sound and, what is more important, the true meaning, of these symbolic words. All names in the Bible and in the ancient world were symbolic (see *Encyc. Bib.*, col. 3,225), and I suspect our Bishops were in fear of the common people understanding the " scriptures " *only too well*, were the names properly pronounced. To return to the Lingam-Yoni altar, of which I give several illustrations—this is simply the male and female sex organs in the act of creation, but, of course,

FIG. 17.—MANDA'S BULL WITH LINGAM-YONI ALTAR.

FIG. 18.—SERPENT LINGAM-YONI.

conventionalised through long generations of descent. Being in the act of creating life, it represents the god or " Maha Devâ " (great god), and it may be seen in tens of thousands all over India and the East, sometimes on an ornamental stand caressed by serpents, symbols of sexual passion, as in Eden. Its name, Lingam-Yoni Ling or Lingah, is vernacular for the phallus or male organ, and the " ah," or " am " (properly " om," Lingom, phallus and womb), are, all three,

FIG. 19.

the symbolic term for the female, the " am " or " om " being the original of our word " womb," and hence of " woman "—the " man " who has the " womb." So the woman is represented by M, N, with vowels on either side of the consonant, am or ma, an or na, om or mo (mother), or simply m or n, and the vulgar word (in India) yoni is our word Iona (a little island in Scotland), where the double-sexed religion, the I (pillar, masculine) and the O and Na (feminine twice repeated), was

F

brought to Scotland by Saint Columba, the "Dove." Iona has also the significance, in Greek, of a " dove," and we remember the " Holy Spirit," as a dove, descending on Jesus as he stood in the Jordan being baptised, like Iona, in the sea. All religion is composed of symbolic tales, the " good work " of the priests, to bewilder the people.

This creative double-sex idea is the basis of all names and symbolism in relation to temples, altars, Church architecture, decorations, instruments, clothing, vestments and sacerdotal paraphernalia of worship in all countries.

Even the word paraphernalia may be simply palaphernalia, as all church utensils were phallic of origin, and be derived from Pala, as phalli were carried in all religious processions ; R and L are always interchangeable, so we have a word, palaphernalia, especially applicable to the equipment and adornment of a church, from pala and " phero," " to bring " or " carry," with the Roman terminal " alia," applied to all processions, phallic feasts, such as Vulcanalia, Fornicalia, Bacchanalia, Maternalia, etc., and it may truly be said of all church paraphernalia that they are entirely phallic. Dome, nave, spire, pulpit, tower, pallium, cross, pyx, are all purely phallic names, so that palaphernalia, or paraphernalia, is a term very applicable to the impress of the pala or phallus borne by the church architecture, utensils and dress. I have dealt with this pretty fully in my "Christianity" and my "Sex Symbolism."

Our Bible and religion are phallic throughout, yet not one person in a thousand knows the meaning of that adjective; in fact, English women blush and men frown at the mention of the word sex; so it is difficult to tell them anything about the gods they worship. Not so the nations who evolved our Bible. It was their entire gospel of eternal life, the eternal reproduction of life. through the sex organs, this combination being their most sacred representation or symbol of the Maha Devâ, great god, creator and upholder of life. Our Christian church architecture, vestments, and furniture are saturated with this "phallic" idea and nomenclature, as are the Mahomadan, Indian, Chinese and Central American religions; in fact, the succession of life through the reproductive organs is admitted by all students of religions to be the only basis for the religious idea of eternal life. The phallus is always symbolised by the serpent all over the world.

We must now become acquainted with the method used by the Romans for the application of this double-sexed creative idea to all religious subjects. The Persians had their legend that Yima, the Creator-on-Earth, was given a " piercer," or dagger, and a " ring " with which to create all life. These, of course, represented the male and female organs, and their conjunction or marriage is symbolised to-day by passing the finger of the person being married (that is of the woman, and " married " is French for " husbanded ") through a ring—imitative of the purpose of marriage, the " life combination " in the god-like act of new life creation.

To return to our early symbolism.

Any upright thing represented the male organ— a post (pala in Hindee), rendered pillar in English, or pole, pale, pile, pilaster, pillar, pestle, and so on [pestilence is caused by an evil condition of the pessil, Hebrew for pestle, and stands for the phallus or male organ], and is symbolically represented by a tree stem, and realistically by a carefully carved stone pillar, the lad, lat, pala, or sul, of India—the mother of religion and religious words—the " rock that begat thee " of Scripture, the " Tsur " of the Hebrews (derived from the Hindoo Sul), the " Rock of our salvation " of the Bible, to which all ancient, and even modern nations prayed (the Cross is the phallus), as they still do in India and the East. We have adopted

the more complete though crude and formal
model of the male reproductive organ—the Cross
—to which to address our prayers, and which

FIG. 20.—A CHRISTIAN CROSS ON A PAGAN
PHALLUS.

women adore, as the symbolic representation of
the Creator (as it virtually is), being the complete,
triple, creative organ of man. I give in Fig. 1

an illustration of a good example of the phallic pillar, still standing in the Bubdown hills, near Dorchester, celebrated in a poem, with an illustration of the pillar, in the *Illustrated London News* in December, 1900, by our grand literateur, Thomas Hardy, O.M., as the " Lost Pyx," and several others more complete, showing the triple organ.

FIG. 21.—ALSACE.

(Figs. 21 to 24.) Pyx is a synonym for the phallus, as pox is for its disease. There are hundreds of thousands of these " Rocks of Salvation " all over Europe, Asia, Africa and America, as illustrated in my " Christianity "—there are over 400 in Cornwall alone—and tens of thousands of small models like our crosses (they are symbolically the same) have been dug up by excavators on the sites of ancient temples and towns. Schliemann

FIG. 22.—SARDINIA.

FIG. 23.—IRELAND.

found them in cities lying three or four successive layers, even to the seventh, under classic Troy, the city of the beautiful Helen, the *motif* of Homer's great work.

Thousands of small models have also been

Fig. 24.—Kerloaz, Brittany.

found round all ancient temple sites, such as that of Paestum in Italy, in fact, all over Europe, Asia, and lately in America also. The reader should also study Colenso's great work, where he traces the cross as a universal symbol of religious adoration back to the epoch of the cave men, when men were scarcely human.

The pillar figured at page 5 from Hardy's poem shows that circumcision was practised, or at least taught, in Britain. Such pillars figured in all old religions from " China to Peru," and Central America shows as many as Europe or Asia. (Colenso on " Crosses," see my " Sex Symbolism in Religion," Vol. I, p. 297.) Colenso wrote "of" the several " varieties of the cross, St. George, St. Andrew, Maltese, Greek, Latin, etc., etc., there is not one amongst them the existence of which may not be traced to the remotest antiquity " " The Pentateuch Examined," Vol. VI, p. 113]. The Scriptures frequently refer to the " Rock that begat thee " (Deut. XXXII, 18, and Genesis XXXIII, 20) as the god, and it is expressed in Hebrew by the word " Tsur " or " Rock of my Salvation," derived from the Hindoo "Sul," or phallic column. R and L are the same letter. This word Tsur is the basis of a great host of Hebrew words and religious names, as we shall see. The Hindoo word Pala, for the male organ, also gave rise to many words and names in the ancient world, as these pillars or palas were erected in every town and village, especially at " cross " roads or ferry " crossings " of rivers, so that the passers-by might pray to it for a safe journey and correct guidance. The Romans used both Tsur and Pal to construct hundreds of artificial names in their Bible. It acquired the name of a cross, as it was always at "crossing" places. It was at first no "cross" in India, but a plain phallic pillar of wood or stone, as in this fancy picture of the virgin of the rocks— "Rock that begat thee" (Fig. 25). It was left for the more western nations, like the Romans, to add a crosspiece to the simple phallic pillar, on which to give directions, and so to represent the complete male life producer phallus and testes —biblical "rod of God and two stones," the complete male organ which Moses placed in the female ark, thus producing the complete god or creator of life, IHOH. The triple male organ thus symbolised is equally represented by the " broad arrow " and the Prince of Wales' feathers, triple

FIG. 26.   FIG. 27.   FIG. 28.   FIG. 29.

articles, and the Fleur-de-lys of France, the Trident of Neptune, the Trisul and Tri-moortee of

India, and so on, all symbolical of the creative nature of man's triple organ. The Hindu " Sul," as in the " Trisul," creative symbol, is the original of the Tsur, the " Rock that begat thee " of the Hebrews, which word, split into Tur and Sur and other modifications, is the central particle in hundreds of names in the Old Testament. All the names in the Old Testament are, as the *Encyc. Bib.* tells us, composed with a special meaning, generally phallic, which practically makes all those kings, holy men, etc., into gods or life-creators, as will be seen in later chapters. " Each of the many names of persons in the Bible must, of course, have had some special meaning " (*Encyc. Bib.*, col. 3,271). That is my argument.

In India the stone pillars, or lingam altars, are still made to flow with oil, which is called, in Hebrew, " semen," seed—a Roman word showing the Roman origin of the imaginary Hebrew's ideas, which demonstrates that the cross with its " arms " signified the male life producer—the " Rod of God " and " two stones " of Moses (Ex. XXV, 16), which he put in the Ark (see my " Sex Symbolism," Vol. I, p. 44). Arnobius, a " Christian " writer of about 300 A.D., wrote, " when I spied an anointed stone or one bedaubed with olive oil as if some person resided in it, I

addressed myself to it and begged blessings."
That is still the universal and very ancient custom
in India, and all over the world among primitive
religionists, as is amply proved by my friends
(alas, no more !), Dr. Oman and Sir Geo. Birdwood,
and also in the exhaustive writings of Major-
General Forlong, Sir Richard Burton, and Sir
Harry Johnston, and hundreds of writers on the
customs of eastern lands, which I have consulted
during a long life.   Sir George Birdwood told the
Society of Arts that " this can be witnessed every
day and at every turn in India " (*Soc. of Arts
Journ.*, 30th Dec., 1910, and 1st Oct., 1911).

.[Major-General Forlong's many volumes form
one of the greatest of expositions of religious
symbolism and practices in the world's literature,
and give examples of every form of phallism.]
If no pala or lingam has been already erected,
the traveller erects a stone (as did Jacob at Luz)
and anoints it with oil (significantly called
" semen " in Hebrew, but a purely Roman word)
and prays to it for good fortune.   Jacob, after
erecting his stone, said " This is El, god of Isra
El," a priestly explanatory remark, inserted by
the scribe for his readers' benefit, as how could
anyone have reported overhearing Jacob making
this formal statement to himself when he was

alone? Of course, it is only a priest's explanation to the reader. The Bible is full of these familiar remarks, which could be known only to the speaker, showing that the whole Bible is pure fiction.

" Each of the many names of persons in the Bible must, of course, have had some special meaning " (*Encyc. Bib.*, col. 3,271). I quite agree, as the Bible is a " composed " book, not a history of natural growth. But does it not occur to these learned—if rather unimaginative professors—that if many of the principal names and statements in our mysterious Bible (secretly produced by the Romans) were invented, as the *Encyc. Bib.* says, then the whole story (utterly uncorroborated in history) with its gods, apostles, prophets, angels and others, who were mere " names," and its silly " miracles," (" childish " is the word used in the *Encyc. Bib.*), suddenly produced as the " Word of God," written to replace the " Old Gods "—is not equally a figment of the priestly imagination. I assert that it was written and imposed on us by the Romans, as will be quite clear to readers who will peruse my arguments to the end. The names are a crucial point, as without names no story can be told, so if the names are fictitious, so is the story. My researches prove that it is an entirely artificial composition, produced by Rome for political purposes.

I have found, as I show in this essay, that the important names are entirely fictitious, in fact, that they are manufactured from a code founded cleverly on the symbolic names and literature of the sex organs, and that the priests' occupation and trade was "High Place," Bom, or Brothel keeping. The *Encyc. Bib.* writers, (especially Dr. Cheyne), are not quite fair in their remarks—always trying to keep up the character of their own sect. He writes of the worship of Istar leading to " shocking practices," while of " Judah " " Harlotry of *both sexes* " " *was not unknown* " (what more shocking practices could there be?), a purely " special pleading " phrase. The reputed inhabitants of Palestine were, according to the Bible account, amongst the most debased of sex worshippers, but, of course, their pornographic stories were simply paraphrased accounts of what the Romans were themselves practising. What, then, could we expect from a priesthood engaged in letting out Kadeshoth, " maidens for prostitution " (*Encyc. Bib.*, cols. 1,964 and 1,965), in a nation whose men, women, and children took part in the open-air, public, stark-naked, priapic, adulterous orgies, when all bonds of relationship were untied, and sexual intercourse enjoyed in full sunshine in presence of the whole population in the public streets and places of Rome twelve times a year. The men who organised these Saturnalia *wrote our Bible.*

From the root words Pal, Tsur, and El, phallic gods (or Al, Il, or Ol, the same) we have a whole world of men, places, and things in Aramaic, Hebrew, Phœnician, Hindoo, Arabic, Abyssinian, Egyptian, Babylonian, Ninevite, and Persian, which spread all over Europe, and the scribes "rang the changes" on words, making one composition serve several meanings. For instance, the word Eloh, singular of Elohim (band of double-sexed gods), reversed, forms Ohel, the word for their sacred tent or Tabernacle, and their word Torah is composed of Tor, the "rock that begat thee," and Ah, the female particle, thus forming a holy or double-sexed name for their "Law," the holy Torah.

The great Oxford *Encyc. Bib.*, in col. 3,275, tells us that "a considerable number of names in the O.T. must be considered as fictitious," and instances (col. 3,281) Elizur, "god is a rock," or simply "god-rock," identical with altar as above ; again, Elizur (Numb. I, 5, and II, 10) is

FIG. 30.

Here is a god-rock (" Rock that begat thee ") seen through the omega (great womb), and the phallus is crowned by a cross, showing that the cross and phallus are the same, and this long before Christianity.

reversed to make Zuriel (Numb. III, 35), and most of the Bible names are made in this way.

The *Encyc. Bib.* concludes that the patriarchs down to Abraham are "invented" (col. 3,275). "Some of the personages (chiefs of the tribes) had no existence" (col. 3,275), and so on, till nearly all the Bible "facts" are shown to be fables, as I have always maintained. The N.T. is treated in the same way by the writers of the *Encyc. Bib.*, who say that Paul's writings and voyages are entirely apocryphal (col. 3,625), and that we have no knowledge of the "life activities or even of the existence of Paul" (cols. 3,627 and 3,630; col. 3,625). With this I am heartily in agreement.

But does it not occur to these learned (if somewhat unimaginative) professors, that, if some of the principal names are "invented" (as in all popular novels), then the whole story is invented, as, without the personalities or names no story could be told? The stories are as artificial as the names and "God's Word" is as true as "Travellers' Tales," and a product of the priestly imagination. Besides, these stories or similar tales have been evolved by all savage tribes in the infancy of their development, as they are the great essentials of the priest's power over his dupes.

G

In inventing words for their fictitious history and its imaginary personnel the priests employed combinations of the names of the sex organs as representing "Holy" or God-like creative power and Kings adopted the same plan—Assurbanipal for instance, Sur, the "Rock," son of "Pal," the phallus.

The word pala gave rise to the names of many royal insignia and ecclesiastical constructions, and is the basis of the words Palestine and Philistine, which names completely disappear in the New Testament, showing that they were entirely the product of the priestly pen, and could be made to appear and disappear like puppets. No traveller and no geographer of contemporaneous history knows or writes of either Palestine or Philistine. They were priestly fables. Pala becomes "Pul" (Assyrian King's name) and, with Pit, the female organ, becomes pulpit, the Holy box from which our clergy speak as did the Israelites of old. The "Stan" (Persian for land or place) gave Palestine, Philistine, and also gave "Palatine," the name of the holy hill in Rome, where the "Palace" was erected, and in which the "mace," a club-shaped shaft or phallus like the "club" of Hercules, was carried in all royal processions, just as huge phalli are still carried in religious processions in India (and formerly in Rome). It was, and is, representative of the god-power which produced all the miracles of Moses, and which was the " rod " or phallus of God, with the two " stones " in the female ark, the whole representing the creative god. This rod was found by Moses in Midian—a purely Roman word (in the " middle " part), and it immediately turned into a live serpent, erecting itself, a true phallus. It is variously named mâté, matiola, matia and mashia or mashie (golf club), and finally " mace," for short, with the usual incorrect pronunciation of the letter A in English. Of course, the rod of God, mâté, which turned into a serpent, was the phallus, and hence many writers state that the mace is a phallic symbol, as I now prove. It also forms the name of the supposed writer of the first Gospel, Maté, Latin Matteus, French Matthieu, English Matthew, thus connecting the Moses history with the first chapter of the Gospels. Palestine, as the name of a land, was utterly unknown till publicly created about 700 A.D. by the Romans, as the scene in which their new ecclesiastical drama was to be played, and, although a small barren country, it was divided in a shadowy way into independent provinces, Philistia, Canaan, Judah,. Israel, Bashan, and so on, rendering impossible the idea of a great rich kingdom like Solomon's.

It was composed of narrow valleys and barren mountains, which could maintain but a scanty population, as I have already pointed out.

Travellers like Herodotus, who traversed this land twice (from Asia Minor to Egypt and return) make no mention of Palestine nor of any clan called Hebrews, and recent excavations by explorers under Mr. Fisher, of Philadelphia University, have laid bare great Egyptian palaces and barracks for soldiers *on both sides of the Jordan and at Beisan*, at the extreme north of Palestine, at the natural gateway to Tyre, so that all Palestine was a mere province of Egypt with a very scant, poor population, and any phantom set of tribes might be staged there without question. There has not been found *one letter or word* of Hebrew in all Palestine—although minute search has been made—neither on rock inscriptions, nor on stone, wood, or papyrus, nor even on clay or leather tablets, by explorers after explorers, including great Egyptologists and special Hebrew scholars and soldiers, such as the painstaking, but latterly tragic figure of Lord Kitchener, who spent some years of investigation there.

So Hebrew was a bastard language of no natural birth, an artificial language and script invented by the *Romans* to form a Bible on which to base their new " Roman Universal Religion " (Catholic means "universal)," through which they hoped to cement their huge and heterogeneous empire and to rule it. All inscriptions or letters found in Palestine are in cuneiform or Egyptian hiero-glyphics, so the Hebrew kingdom is a myth of the Roman Church created for political purposes.

The composers of the Old Testament were prepared for this, and they tell us that Jerusalem was held by the Jebusites, as stated in several texts, and any Hebrew there lived " under the Jebusites," as stated in Judges III, 5, "and worshipped their gods." But in Judges and Ezra we are plainly told that they were controlled by the " people of the land " (Ezra IV, 23), and inter-married with the " Canaanites, Hitties, Amorites. Perizzites, Hivites and Jebusites " (who held Jerusalem) " and served their " (all these tribes') " gods," an ever-varying evanescent worship of new gods; but more probably they were, as to-day, living on sufferance as an inferior race; so even in their own supposed holy scripture it is shown that they never were a nation, and all Solomon's " glory " and his thousand million pounds worth of gold and silver were ridiculous myths, as Colenso so long ago proved, or as shown in another light in my " Christianity " and " Sex Symbolism."

Palestine was an Egyptian province until Rome conquered Egypt; then Rome governed it as a part of her conquests.

Nearly all the Roman Emperors claimed to be Sons of God (like Jesus), through the " converse " of their mothers with a god, as was told of the Virgin Mary. For the long list of " sons of god " see my " Sex Symbolism " or my " Christianity." Even the famous Emperor Julius Cæsar (Kâisar or Kyesar is the proper pronunciation), who conquered France and Britain, and who from his clear, logical writings and his clean-cut intellectual face, like a clever city solicitor, as seen in his bust in marble in the British Museum, seems incapable of any fraudulent humbug, claimed that he was the son of a god, through the " converse " of his mother with a god; and nearly all the Roman Emperors made the same claim, *and they were believed.*

This pala, pole, pestle, or phallus, was the " Piercer " or dagger (observe the supremacy of the letter P or Ph in all these and allied words. " Pessel " is " phallus " in Hebrew, and is still used in Scotland by rude boys, pronounced peezel), and, associated with a ring, which it pierced, it was the means by which Yima created life in the Persian legend. It is a universal symbol of eternal life, and our conventional form of it is the cross, which many of us worship.   Let us see how universally this word pala, phallus, pole, pale, pile, or pul (always P) was used wherever it had been erected as a god, to whom prayers were addressed, as stated by the Christian teacher Arnobius to be the universal custom.   Palal means " to pray," but it is composed of pal, the male organ, and Al, god, telling that the phalla is the God, cryptically.   The pala or phallus was the " love " organ, and was, and is still, worshipped as the god by some people, so the modern "·God is love " is literally true.   The Greeks, who were great corrupters of language, used the Phi, Φ, (pronounced as " fee," not as " fie "—the English are worse than the Greeks), the phallic letter *par excellence*, as it includes the two sex members *in coitu*), in place of P or Pi, and they changed the A into I or Y, and added an affix (which they used lavishly) and so produced " Philip," " the loving one," and " Phyllis," the " loving maid " of poetry, although they still called the organ phallos.   They added ".is " to many words, making Seraph into Serapis, Isa into Isis, and their use, of " phil " instead of the Hindoo " pal " has given rise to about 200 " philos " in modern dictionaries, as " lovers of," such as " philosophers," lovers of wisdom, " philtre," a " love " potion ; and doctors

have named the worst sexual disease, " syphilis,"
the " with love " disease. The letter Φ, erroneously pronounced " fie," is used by mothers in
rebuking children for any " exposure " of person
by saying " Fie, for shame."

Those who composed the Bible used both the
Hindoo "pala" and the Greek "phil" to name
the principal actors in their entirely fictitious tale,
calling the main country of their drama Palestine,
and that of their fictitious enemies Philistia, both
derived from the Hindee "pala" or "phala." The
name Philistine could at that time be applied to
any nation, even to England, as they were all
pillar, pala, or phallus worshippers, and so they
were " Phallustines " or " Philistines," worshippers
or devotees of the pala, phallus, or philis—witness
the phallic columns in hundreds in Britain, in fact
all over the world, as in my illustration from
Dorsetshire, and, as I have detailed in my
" Christianity, the Sources of its Teaching and
Symbolism," a world-wide study of all religious
symbolism. Besides, the Cross is the phallus.

These phalli, found everywhere, all over the
world, in both hemispheres, teach us two things,
first, that all nations from Japan and China through
Asia and Europe to Central and South America,
and a great part of North America (as I have shown

FIG. 4. DORSET COLUMN

in my other books) worshipped the sex organs as
the fount of all life, and as symbolical of " life "
and the creator or god ; and secondly, that when

FIG. 32.—Christian Cross on a Phallic pillar.

they were rendered active, as in the sexual act of
creation imitated by pouring oil (called " semen,"
a Latin word in the Hebrew Bible) on them, they

represented " the living god," which heard and answered prayer, and caused miracles to happen. The serpent was universally employed as the symbol of the phallus. In legendary lore, Phyllis was changed into an almond (or almond tree)

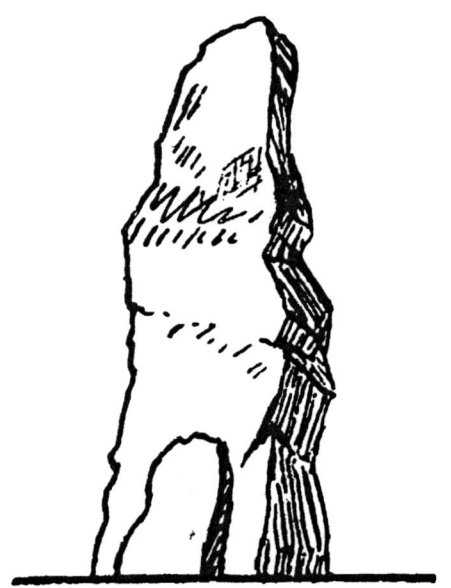

FIG. 33.—Phallic Rock.

Note here that the " Rock that begat thee" was often represented by a rough-hewn or unhewn slabs with two smaller slabs. Here we have that form with the Magdalene. See also pp. 72-76.

and called migdal, from the Greek for "almond," owing to the shape of the female organ (Yima's ring or oval) ; and temple women or sacred harlots were called " Migdalenes " or " Magda-

lenes," hence modern scholars tell us that Mary Magdalene was a temple prostitute, or an " almond " woman. She had " loved much," as was her profession (Luke VII, 47). This was quite a " holy " calling in biblical times, as the Kadeshoth (dedicated women) were attached in great numbers to all temples (in fact the whole temple revenues were derived from prostitution).

The results of this traffic are told symbolically in 1st Sam. 5th and 6th, using the symbolical Ark as representing the womb of a female pudendum. When the Philistines took the Ark of God (God's wife)—God being double-sexed (Elohim, or " El " male, " O " female, " im " plural), and as the Ark is the womb, the passage means taking the sexual use of the Hebrew women to grace the Philistines' temple brothels. In consequence they took " Ophalim in their secret parts " (man-woman disease disguised as " Emerods "), meaning a double-sex disease, (O woman, Phallim male organs), or syphilis. The Philistines made five golden " Emerods," models of the combined sex organs, and five golden mice (male organs, " little secret things of the night ") purely phallic emblems. So the double-sex disease, syphilis, was cured by golden images of the organs involved in sacred prostitution. Jeremiah, being called to his prophetic career, was asked by Jehovah (Jer. I, 11) " What seest thou ?" and answered, " Rod and almond," certainly not " Rod of an almond tree," as it is dishonestly translated in our Bible. Jeremiah was giving the names of the two sex organs, as from the conjunction of these not only was life continued on earth, but the *entire* revenue of the ecclesiastics was derived from the services of the sacred prostitutes performing the god-like operation of creating new life in their temple cubicles. Jeremiah's answer was really at once the name and description of the Church's operations at that time and down to about 1500 A.D.

As I have said, these temple women, called in Hebrew Kadeshoth, that is, female priests, dedicated to prostitution [there were also Kadeshim, male prostitutes] (see *Encyc. Bib.*), and they were the so-called " holy women " of the New Testament. When the Sun was in "pisces," the fish sign, they were called " nuns "—Babylonian for fishes—a name used for holy women to the present day, perhaps not always dedicated for public use, but probably for the consolation of the celibate clergy, as, wherever monks, priests or ecclesiastical scholars were [or are] gathered together, say, at Galilee for the production of our Bible, there was provided a " nunnery," called in Hebrew "Migdal Nunya," "almond nuns," or "fish." "Migdal" was also used as a tower or "keep," and that was its use, from these women being strictly secluded or kept for the use of the priests and scholars who were creating the Bible, as they are still, under the Roman Pope's *régime*. Their dormitories were called "keeps" or towers (lovers' towers), like our Tower of London, which is not a "tower" but a "keep" (to keep our harbour safe in ancient times), like the buildings for "keeping" or secluding nuns. Migdal is also employed to designate the use by men of their "almonds," and came to be applied to any "secluding place"—"tower" for preference. We must not forget that "tower" is a modification or tur or tsur, the "rock that begat thee," so the tower for secluding nuns was connected in name with the male organ or phallus, tor, from tsur, "the rock that begat thee." Names of the sex organs and their symbols were combined, as in the semi-precious stone Opal—"O" being the usual symbol or letter from the Persian legend for the woman's organ, and "pal," the Hindee for the male "pillar," opal being a transparent hydrated silica with fissures so fine that they decompose the light and give gleams of fiery light, and so represent fire or man, while the unfissured silica is clear like water—woman's symbol. This stone is set in the breast-plate of the Jewish High Priest, and represented a creative name of the god —being double-sexed or Hermaphroditic.

This compound holy word was applied as a sacred name to cities where important temples existed, as in Sevastopol, Adrianopol (the Emperor Adrian's "sacred" city), Constantinople (Constantine's city), and the same sacred combination was applied as the primary part of town names, as Opalin, Opalaca, Opalenitza—no doubt sacred towns in early times.

Another phallically-named stone, also one of those set in the Hebrew High Priest's breast-plate, the Onyx, O (or On or Om) the yoni or womb, and the cross X representing the male, joined by Y, which is U in Greek, hence female, or I in Latin, which is male, probably chosen to represent double-sex or god, repeating the double-sex or "god symbol" in the middle of the word—the old priests delighting in multiplying the name or symbol of the Deity by all sorts of cryptic words and letters. So "opal" and "onyx" have similar meanings. We get into touch here with the use of the cross or X in phallic words, as in pyx for the phallus, and pox for its disease.

It is significant that "ovum" (egg) contains

all the female phallic letters in it and its plural
" ova." O, U, and V represent the female organ,
and " um " or " om," are our word womb, again
female ; while the plural "ova" gives the grammatical "A" or Ah feminine in Hebrew, so in the
" ovum " a female product, we have the entire
battery of female symbols included. This is
not accidental, as priests were always seeking
such " secret signs." Egg, in Greek Oon, contains
the two forms of O, Omega and Omikron, big and
little O, and the female N. As L and R are
interchangeable—in fact, some nations, such as the
Chinese and Japanese, and the ancient Egyptians,
have, or had, only one sign for these curious palatal
sounds—so we find pal and pul, changed to " par,"
" pore," and " pur," applied to hundreds of
names, in India especially, such as Singapore,
(China town), Mirzapore, Nagpur, Midnapur,
Palampore, Cawnpore, etc. Palampore, Pal-am-
pur being one female between two male particles,
in fact the Hindoo " pala " was ubiquitous, and
India is the " Mother of Religions." The same
word was applied by the Hebrews to their two great
feasts, which were, and still are, phallic orgies in
some communities—" Aaron had made them naked
unto their shame "—such as were common all
over the East till long after the Christian Era,

and still practised secretly in many countries by
Jews, especially in Europe, and savages in all
tropical countries, as on the Amazon river [see
the worship of Jurapari by the Uapés, page 41
in this book], which I describe as an example of
these feasts everywhere. The Jewish Spring feast,
to celebrate the " passing-over " of the sun to the
summer (paradise), half of the year, was called the
feast of " Purim " (*i.e.*, Phallim)—" im " is plural
in Hebrew—and that of the Autumn equinox the
feast of " Kipurim " (on account of phalli),
although the Bible represents it as a celebration
of the passing out of Egypt—the pass-over. These
feasts are still common with the African aborigines,
and were called " Hags " by the Hebrews, as
when they demanded to be allowed by Pharaoh
to make a " three days' journey " into the desert
to hold a " hag " to the IHOH of their Aléim, *i.e.*,
to the " double-sexed leader of their stone pillar
gods." This " Hag " was a triple orgy of flesh,
meat, wine, and sex, or, as the *Encyc. Bib.* says
(col. 1,513) " ate, drank and *made merry*," the
last always a euphuism for sexual and incestuous
intercourse, when " all bonds of relationship were
loosed." We have, or had in my youth, a dim
shadow of it in Scotland with much love-making,
described by Burns in none too veiled language,

called " Hogmanay," or in Hebrew " Hag-manah," meaning " the day of feast of the numberer," to celebrate the end of the harvest gathering—or it may be of the year—the days of toil being numbered, and the fruits of all their toil "ingathered." It was held in Scotland on 31st December.

These Hebrew " Hags " were fairly frequent, and like those of the Romans, " all bonds were loosed," a phrase applying to family relationship if it were desired, and still practised in places uninfluenced by European civilisation, and probably secretly in Europe. Up to the time of Queen Elizabeth, who, as we know, was " none too strait-laced," these excursions into lonely places " to make merry " all night, were universal even in Puritan countries, and Stubbes, a Puritan reformer, tells us that " Fourtie or three score, or a hundred maids goying to the woode over night, there have scarcely the third part returned home againe undefiled " (*Anatomie of Abuses*, fol. 94, London, 1583).

The maypole was also the cause of much " merry " rejoicing, exactly like the procession with huge phalli in India to-day, which I describe, and when it was cut and brought from the forest and danced to on its way to the village, disorderly scenes with " licentious happenings " continued

H

till daylight.   I saw a very pretty sight at a Board School in Fulham Road in the West of London, where the schoolmaster or mistress had a fine maypole with its coloured ribbons, and the children were very happy weaving chequered patterns, many of them with coloured paper caps.   It was extremely pretty and joyous, but I never saw it again.   I suppose some puritanical member of the School Board declared it " pagan," and one more touch of sunshine in the children's lives was extinguished.   We all ought to rejoice in the return of Spring, without going " too far."

We have the same use of the " pala " or pole root in Metropolis, Acropolis, inverted Phalakra or Polacra, etc., and timid scholars translate Phalakra as " bald-head," whereas its literal translation is the top or " point of the phallus," which the shaved head of the priest is intended to represent, as shown in this figure of a priest with his " phalakra " inserted through the yoni or female part of the Egyptian " ankh," embroidered on his pallium (phallic cloak), the arrangement representing the god, or life-creative pair in the act of producing life—or a god.   The Hebrew Bible uses another word of very widespread application, viz., Tsur, the word in the Bible for the " Rock that begat thee," or the god-column, a true phallus, well illustrated in Hardy's " Lost Pyx " [Fig. 1]. That word has sunk into the languages of all countries, from Western Asia to the Atlantic. This word, Tsur, is no doubt derived from the Hindoo " Sul," a pole or column, sometimes represented as a complete male organ, the trisul or trident of Neptune. From Tsur

FIG. 35.—FATHER CONFESSOR ANKH.

it sometimes takes the T initial letter, and sometimes the S, as the Hebrew letter Tsadi, is used, and Ts or Tz were sounds seldom used in the greater number of languages, especially when used at the beginning of a word. So instead of Tsur [which is Tzar, the sacred Emperor of Russia, which made him a creative god] we have words utilising the T initial, such as tower, tor in English, and in the Bible we have words beginning with T using all the vowels, as in Tar, Ter, Tir, Tor, Tur and Tyr, and others utilizing the S sound, such as Sar, Ser, Sir, Sor, Sur and Syr, in names of men and places. (See Appendix).

Then, as "L" and "R" are identical letters or represented by one sign in Egypt and several eastern countries, we have (still from Tsur) Sal, Sel, Sil, Sol, Sul, Syl, and so on; and further, S becomes "Sh," then we have words like Shalmanezer, Shulamite, where S has become Sh, and the R has become L, both softened, going on to all the vowels as before, as Shalim, Sheleph, Shilo, etc. In this way was all the great list of thousands of names in the O.T. created—imaginary gods, kings, and common people being created for the priests' story as required. I will treat this more fully later on. The result was that the names of old gods who were generally " creative," that is, double-sexed, were used—with slight alterations—to form, in our Bible, the names of patriarchs, kings, priests and prophets, and places, and all the paraphernalia of religious worship, and also for ordinary men and women, and new names were easily coined when required. Not only were these imaginary gods and personages

FIG. 37. RUBEN'S MAGDALENE

double-sexed in name, but this double-sexed or creative idea was applied to everything connected with religion—priests' vestments, sacred vessels, church architecture, and to the services and

FIG. 36.—EGYPTIAN VERSION OF EVE
TEMPTING ADAM.

Here the Magdalene is naked and defenceless, the condition of all nuns, fish-women, or sacred harlots, body and soul in the priests' power. Her foot is on a skull—death—the result of her "profession," and the serpent means the phallus associated with a skull—death her only release, yet she is represented in Egypt as the author of all evil.

miracle plays performed in the temples, as detailed in my " Christianity."

We must not forget that harlotry was the chief, perhaps the only source of wealth of the priests of the old world, and thousands of sacred prostitutes were kept at all the famous sacred shrines, and "converse" with the holy women, or prostitutes, was a sacred act. This traffic flourished vigorously about the beginning of the Christian era, but it always existed, (see the " Syrian Goddess " of Lucian), while in Europe Bishops had harems and travelled with their concubines, and the Bishop of Liége had seventy concubines, while nunneries were like huge brothels and infanticide flourished up till the 18th century. One Bishop had over 70 acknowledged children, and Lecky tells us that nunneries were simply brothels. (Lecky, Vol. I, pp. 419, 440, etc., and Vol. II, pp. 217, 219, 330, 331).

Lecky quotes from " the vast mass of evidence which has been collected from the writings of Catholic divines and from decrees of Catholic councils " during the space of many centuries ; so the descriptions in the Bible from the complaints of the prophets are an exact replica of what was going on in Rome and Constantinople, during the creation of the Bible, and in Europe till quite recent times. In earlier times, of course, morality as we understand it, that is, regulated sexual intercourse by marriage only, was utterly unknown, as there were feasts with public celebrations at stated intervals, when public sexual intercourse was a public duty and a " confession of faith " ; and where and when the sacred prostitutes were stripped naked and committed the " great sacrifice " with the men of the town openly and publicly as a profession of Orthodoxy. These women were called " Kadeshoth," consecrated women (singular Kadeshah), and there were also Kadeshim (singular Kadesh), male prostitutes, for debasing practices, attached to all temples ; these words meaning men and women consecrated to prostitution and unnatural vices, under the blessings of the priests, who pocketed all the fees for the upkeep of their temples [centres of vice and deadly diseases]. In India the sacred prostitutes were called Palaki, from pala, the male organ, with the female determinant KI, just as the male god was Devâ, root of our " divine," and his female consort Devaki. The almond was the favourite symbol of the *membrum femininum* and Mary Magdalene was not Mary of the town of Magdala (Almond) but, being a temple harlot, (as the Church of England *Encyc. Bib.* admits), she was Mary of the " Almond "—symbol for the *membrum femininum* indicating her calling. We see its use in Jeremiah I, 11, as I have already stated, where Jeremiah tells IHOH that he visualises his profession as that of " Rod and Almond," " regulator of temple prostitution." Hosea is commanded to " Go, take unto thee a wife of the whoredoms," and we know from old writers, Lucian for instance, that temple women were readily sought in marriage, "no one disdaining a connection with such persons " (*Encyc. Bib.*, col. 3,615). " Saint " Augustine commanded ladies to attend the " Eucharist," and to wear " clean linen," as the "Holy Kiss " was administered, and it was this "free trade " in private prostitution by the new Christian Church which aroused the priests of the older temples—with their official Kadeshoth and Kadeshim—to violent denunciation. The Christians were destroying the Hebrew priests' revenues, as the Christians were all free lovers and paid no fees. Sodomy was also a part of the Priest's Holy Office, by Kadeshim, " consecrated " men.

PART II

HAVING now gained an idea of the old world and its customs about the time when Rome conceived her plan for cementing her ramshackle empire—having found that, however easy it was to conquer small uncivilised nations one by one, it was a much more difficult task to hold them all simultaneously—she began to seek for some method other than that of armed force, for holding control of the lands she had conquered.

Realising the power of a united priesthood, under Roman control, as a cement to hold her conquests, she decided to impose a universal religion on the countries she had conquered, and thus draw the revenue from the profession of the sacred prostitutes from a broader basis.. The revenue from prostitution was more regular, certain, and ubiquitous, than that from any other source of wealth for the State. For the more ignorant tribes they had a form of serpent worship (the serpent is the universal emblem of the phallus), so they could introduce a serpent worship of great antiquity ; as the *Encyc. Bib.* tells us, " The Israelites worshipped a quite peculiar symbol of the Deity, the brazen serpent, " Nehushtan." "It stood in the Temple, and incense was offered to it." This was simply the phallic symbol universally worshipped. In ancient Rome the prosperity of the coming year was judged by the offering of food to the sacred serpents by perfectly nude maidens. But, of course, the great attraction would be the sacred prostitutes, who, says Frazer in his " Golden Bough," were " set apart, at puberty from the households in which they grew up, for prostitution according to a custom [still extant] which ranges from the Gold Coast to Tahiti," fully trained in the then honourable profession of religious prostitution.

The *Encyc. Bib.* refers to this in several paragraphs, such as at col. 837, " The offer of the body in honour of the Deity prevailed widely in Northern Semetic religions," " a special class of temple harlots was retained," " commerce with them was a religious act " [with fees payable to the priests], " the hire was sacred and brought into the *treasury* of the god." Of course, the god was simply the State. Fine words, but the " priests' official brothel " would be a shorter description, and more appropriate. This pharasaic phraseology about prostitution in the *Encyc. Bib.* is inhuman and disgusting, " the offer of the body in honour of the Deity." What Deity ? They were simply " white slaves," dedicated to the most abominable traffic. They made no " offers "; they simply did what the priests commanded them, and when they were wrecked by disease, they were put " out of the way "—generally by being smothered. " Commerce " with them was a religious act, forsooth, " the hire was sacred, and brought into the treasury of the god "; but coming to more modern times, it is all grouped under " filthy sensuality." How these solemn professors can seriously prate about the " offer of the body in honour of the Deity," when these poor victims, dedicated from childhood to this abominable traffic and death, show to what awful depths of hypocrisy the religious views of such acts can lower an educated man. The position of the prostitute is pathetically portrayed by Rubens in this plate (Fig. 37, p. 102)—one of martyrdom, a life of Hell, to satisfy the greed of the male priests and the cupidity of the State. Women's long martyrdom of torture did not count with the soulless State and its priests. The *Encyc. Bib.* ignores the fact that all religions were phallic, with sacred prostitutes, yet tells us that all the places visited by Paul were famous for "filthy sensuality," ignoring the fact that this was the Church's entire source of income (*Encyc. Bib.*, col. 3,615). This "filthy sensuality" was the Church's whole business and source of revenue in all countries. As their income arose from this traffic, it was no wonder that all the symbolic names of men, places, and things, in Aramaic, Hebrew, Phœnician, Egyptian, Babylonian, Ninevite and Hindoo, which spread over Europe, were derived from the root words of the sex organs.

The *Encyc. Bib.* further says, "Some of these personages had no existence" (col. 3,275). If some had no existence, how do they prove the existence of others? I assert that they are all creations of the pen. That the Church professors know of the fictitious character of the entire Bible record is proved by their articles. Of course, each writer showed his learning by criticising some special text or texts. But when they had all spoken, one finds that the entire Bible, both Old and New Testaments, is declared to be made up of "sham writings"—"pseudepigrapha," the *Encyc. Bib.* calls them. I cannot detail that, as it would take several large volumes to expose the Church's cloaking of its iniquities. But the learned men who wrote the *Encyc. Bib.* missed or rather avoided the whole point, or perhaps turned a "blind eye" to dangerous texts, as a common-sense explanation of the Bible names, sufficient to reveal their true meaning, would be fatal to their whole ecclesiastical business. The Bible names were almost entirely derived from phallic (or sex organ) roots, and dealt with the god-like idea of the everlasting renewal of life by the conjunction of the two sex organs, or the everlasting reproduction of life, amounting to "everlasting life" in the mass. But from its naturalistic derivation from phallic roots Mrs. Grundy would call the Bible a "shamelessly immoral book" from beginning to end.

The god's own most sacred name, to attempt to pronounce which was punishable with death, [African, mumbo-jumbo], but which we courageously but erroneously call "Jehovah" [and we are not struck dead], and which is composed of four letters of "unutterable sacredness" IHOH, is the expression, most complete, of the conjunction of the male and female organs in creating life, so extensively practised in the Church brothels. The writers of the *Encyc. Bib.* well know the truth of what I write, but its publication, or even admission, would disrupt their Church, hence their silence on this burning question, "What sort of a god do we worship?" [Our New Testament god,

Jesus, has a similar origin, as we shall see]. We will take a simple example from which I shall endeavour to show how completely the phallic ideas were used to build up all Bible names.

In the *Encyc. Bib.* we are told in cols. 4,284–4,285 that Sarah—Abraham's wife and sister (doubly feminine) was a princess or a queen (Babylonian), and that her name and her father's name, Terah, are god-names, and therefore she is a god, like her father, but she is also stated to have been a goddess, in fact the Babylonian Istar (col. 4,285). (I have no inclination to seek for such far-fetched impersonations.) This is quite true, as all gods were double-sexed, and so was Sarah. I have shown on p. 101 that the word " tsur," the "rock that begat thee," the phallus, originally derived from Sul, the phallic column of India, is divided into two root-words, tur and sur, and by substitution of various vowels (which are always liquid), and of R for L (a world-wide similarity), is metamorphosed into a great list of words used to invent the special names necessary to compose the Bible story. I give details later in this volume of the vast creation of names, about 7,000 of them, to compose the Bible allegory, all derived from Hindoo roots. So, sur and tur become " sar and tar," " ser and ter," " sir and tir," and so on through all the alphabetical gamut. Now to return to Sarah.

The name Sarah is made up of sar, the masculine "rock that begat thee," and "ah," the female affix, or particle, so Sarah is double-sexed, and hence a creative god. She is self-fructifying, hermaphroditic, or omphallic, and so can create new life like a god—at least her name declares her to have the god-like quality of creating life. So the *Encyc. Bib.* is quite right, but terribly unorthodox, in saying that Sarah is a god. That this intention is true is proved from another name, Seraiah, meaning that Sera or "Sarah is Iah," or Jehovah, as we erroneously pronounce IHOH. So here Sarah is masculine, and equal to Jehovah. Sarah's father Terah is equally a god, or double-sexed, from "ter," the T initial of "tsur" the rock, and "ah," the feminine determinant or particle, as vowels do not signify, as they were mere dots or small lines and crosses so easily mistaken or displaced. The scribes who composed the Old Testament go on playing on these words and adding the phallic serpent "aph" or "eph," so Sarah and Terah are converted into gods, and their names occur as Teraph and Seraph, or plural as Teraphim and Seraphim idols, images, or gods ; the words mean literally rock serpents, or,

as the rock is the god, god serpent, prayed to by
the Hebrews (Judges XVII, 5, and Isaiah VI, 2),
elsewhere mis-translated " images " (Gen. XXXI,
18 and 34). We remember Rachel stealing her
father's Teraphim (images) (Gen. XXXI, 19–34).
The final " aph " is the serpent, so we find these
two symbolise " man's rock in presence of the
serpent," or sexual passion, in fact the Garden
of Eden story, or the fall of man, which made Eve
the " mother of all living.".

We shall see these symbolically composed names
repeated constantly in Bible names, in fact the
Encyc. Bib. tells us that Bible names are artificial
compositions. For instance, Joseph, a name
which has no J, but is IOseph, English Yoseph,
I, O, male and female (piercer and ring of Yima),
with seph, serpent—again the story of the " fall "
in Eden (man and woman in presence of sexual
passion). The same symbolism was in use in
Egypt, where the " Phara-Oh " (Hindoo " Phala-
O," as R and L are represented by one letter or
sign in Egypt), double-sexed or creative king,
and therefore a god, whose name we ignorantly
pronounce Fair-O, instead of Far-ah-O, is also
called O-Sar, O being female, and Sar the " rock
that begat thee," as in Sarah, O and A (or Ah)
being equally female symbols. Osar was con-

verted into Osiris by the Greeks, who were great corrupters of languages. They also corrupted Isa into Isis, Phallus into Phylis, Seraph into Serapis, after which god we will remember one of the great Alexandrian libraries, the Serapeum, was named, where were stored the great collection of the temple literature of all languages, from which the ideas were obtained to found the Hebrew Bible and its equally artificial Greek, second or New " Testament." The derivatives of tsur have migrated into Britain as " sur " and ". tur," the latter giving us tower, and tor, for a peaked rock, and the " sur " as Sul in Sulgrave Manor, the home of Washington, and other names.

That the Phara-O should be Phalla-O, or better Pala-O, is shown by the fact that the grown-up Egyptians are called fellahs or phallas, plural fellahim, to this day, meaning " males," as does our word " fellow," as in a " leud fellow." The word " pala " also became " peel," and migrated to Scotland and in the " wild west " of Ireland, where " peel towers " (pala turs) were erected. Here we have, far from their origins, two words, " pala," the phallus, and " tor," from " tsur," the " rock that begat thee," rendered into modern words " peel tower " (pala turs), of which there are many in Ireland and some in Scotland. Our great General,

I

Earl Haig of Bemersyde, when presented with an estate in Scotland, found that he was " Lord of the Peel Tower," as there was one of these sacred erections on his estate. These are very high slender towers, too small in diameter to yield chambers of any capacity, more like short factory chimneys than towers, but quite good representatives of the phallus on an immense scale. So Lord Haig has a title far older than his Earldom, and derived from the most ancient Indian and Babylonian sources. Peel is simply pala, of India.

We have the same word in Norway's god " Tor," or Thor, whose " hammer " is no hammer, but a model of the entire male reproductive organ, always a triple form, derived from Tur, " the rock that begat thee." The same mistake was made by Sir Arthur Evans, who, on describing the Minoan symbolism, calls the same " hammer " (symbolised) the " double axe of Minoah," whereas it is simply the same as Tor's hammer or Moses's Rod of God and his two stones which he placed in the Ark. *Axe, Hammer and Cross are identical.*

By the way, Sir Arthur Evans does not explain to us the meaning of the name of the Minoan kingdom. It is simply the ithyphallic (erect phallus) or shameless god Min of Egypt, of which I give examples in a photograph of a shelf of

FIG. 38. EGYPTIAN MIN

The "shameless" or ithyphallic god Min gave rise to a number of god-names on being coupled with the female particle A Ah, or "O" generally spelt men as in Mena, Menah Mino (Crete), and Ammon or Amon, and Oman, but it is most familiar to us when we apostrophise him at the end of our prayers as "Amen" so we address our final appeal to the "shameless" ithyphallic god and his female counterpart A-men.

gods of Egypt in the British Museum, and the ring O, the universal sign of woman, as in Yima's "piercer and ring," making the word Min-O, like the Egyptian kings Phara-O, or Phala-O, and this, combined with the name of the Bull Taurus, gave Minotaur, their sacred double-sexed bull-god. (I beg to thank the Director of the British Museum for permission to photograph several of the Museum's unique exhibits.) The Minoans do not seem to have made images of the Min god as a creative or double-sexed god, but they revelled in the sight of fruitful woman, well provided with mammary glands, to support the "Be fruitful and multiply" instinct, as will be seen from this photograph of their serpent goddess, who flourished two serpents as symbols of a phallic religion. The breasts are female, the serpents male, again making a double-sexed symbol of the creative god (p. 118).

Thus we see that the sex organs were the embodiment of their idea of a creative god, conventionalised as far as Christianity is concerned by the cross, but fully embodied in the Hebrew most sacred IHOH, which we call Jehovah, but which was so holy that it was death to pronounce it or even to attempt to do so.

But such ideas left out all view of a future life, and hence, all their authority obtained on the basis

of their religion leading to heaven would be lost
by their acceptance. They desired to remain
" Sole vendors of the lore that works salvation,"
and they desired that their Church should be the
only safe guide. The sex organs were their god,
as is, in fact, their symbolic representation, the
male Cross, to-day. We get a very clear key to the
whole method if we consider a few typical names
along with the " most holy " name IHOH, which
we call Jehovah, but to pronounce which was
punished with death. The meaning of the sacred
four letters is quite clear to such modern scholars
as have some knowledge of the origin of alphabetical letters and their use in symbolism. The
sacred names in the Bible are all artificial symbolic
names, but they are all founded on a few letters,
and when these letters' signification is made clear
the names become quite comprehensible to the
initiated. But, the Bible names being nearly all
derived from phallic roots, dealing with the idea
of the god-like attribute of the everlasting renewal
of life by the conjunction of the two sex organs,
our modern orthodox writers are loth to reduce
divine names to such a level. But the matter is
quite simple, and we will get a very clear key to
the method if we consider a few typical names,
along with the " most holy " name IHOH, which

we erroneously call Jehovah, we will soon arrive
at a true explanation of all Bible names. The
ancient priests must have found it inconvenient
to have to explain this sacred unpronounceable
word IHOH, so they cut the matter short by
condemning to death anyone attempting to pronounce it, or even for asking any questions con-
cerning it.

The chief function of a god is as creator, especially as creator of that great mystery " life," and
this " four-letter " title minutely but secretly
describes the nature of the life-creating god.

First, it must contain letters which indicate a
name which expresses the two sexes in one god,
that is, it must be " Hermaphroditic " or " Omphallic " (from " Om," womb, and " phallos," the
male organ) and so we have the ring and dagger,
or " door of life " and its " piercer," in the IO,
the beginning of so many Bible names, such as
Joseph, which should be Ioseph, and is still pronounced Yoseph in Egypt, Palestine, Persia, and
India, and in fact all over the East. Of course,
the vowels vary as in Yusuph, Yasaph, etc., but
its meaning is male and female in the presence
of the serpent—sexual passion—the story of
Eden. But the Roman composers of our Bible
knew that something more was required to produce,

or reproduce life, as they saw from the inability of Eunuchs to produce children, and they knew that the " testes " were the secret spring of the Breath of Life, and they damned those who had even accidentally lost the testes or " stones " in the Commandment (IHOH's special Commandment in Deut. XXIII, 1) : " He that is wounded in the stones or hath his privy member cut off shall not enter into the congregation of the Lord " (IHOH), and in Leviticus XXI, 17–20, " Whosoever hath any blemish, let him not approach to offer the food of his god," such as " one who hath his stones broken." [Poor Eunuchs, condemned for the action of their parents]. Now the Hebrew H, the "breath of life " letter representing the ". stones," is placed after the male I (pillar) and is repeated on both right and left sides of the female O, so the Romans probably knew of the ovaries also as a primary source of the new life. So the two H's may stand for the two egg founts of life, the testicles and the ovaries. The word egg, which describes a purely feminine product, is a name which, I think, has been the subject of manipulation by makers of phallic symbolism. In Latin it is " ovum," and we remember that the Latin O, U, and V were cut out in Hebrew and altered to prevent them from giving any hint of being feminine symbols, and were replaced by a little staff. " Ovum " contains all three and also the female symbol *par excellence* M, and its plural, " ova," contains the grammatical feminine terminal letter A, often written " Ah," so the egg or " ovum " sums up all the female letter symbols except N, which is seldom used, and then, as a variant of M. The N is, however, found in the Greek word for " egg," ΩoN (Oon), exhibiting the great and little O's—" omega " and omikron " —and thus emphasising the N as a female symbol, and giving all the female symbolic letters in a female product, the egg. I cannot think that this is accidental. It looks like a very clever and *à propos* introduction of these symbolical words by some popular lexicographer, or through priest scribes. We have a church, now Southwark Cathedral, called " Saint Mary of the Ovaries," in London, but the clerics, ashamed of the name, have " created " it, 1924, " Southwark Cathedral," to " save their faces." The ineffable IHOH was too holy to be pronounced, so the scripture reader said " Adonai " instead—another god name, common in such names as Adonijah, Adoniram, etc. The punishment of death was meted out also to anyone touching, looking into or inquiring as to our monstrance and pyx—the monstrance being an " almond "-shaped or dove-shaped vessel representing woman, or the *membrum femininum*, and the pyx a rod-like article which lay inside the monstrance (or mother), and death was meted out to one of our soldiers by his being hanged, drawn and quartered in sight of the French enemy (for having touched the monstrance and pyx) before the battle of Agincourt.

Phallic pillars like that in Dorsetshire were called pyxes, as in Thomas Hardy's poem (on this very column), entitled the " Lost Pyx." It is also spelt " pix," as in our word " pixie," for a " sprite " (spirit), and P is the universal phallic letter, and the pillar I stands for the male organ everywhere, while the cross or X (✝) is the universal " mark " or symbol for the complete male organ (Colenso), so we have here an intensely male phallic word, held to be most intensely sacred, as all oaths were sworn on the phallus, as when Abraham swore his servant (Gen. XXIV, 9), as eastern men do to this day, or when we swear on the cross, which is the complete male organ, Rod of God, and two stones of Moses's Ark. But without the " stones " no creation of life could be made, so Moses put the Rod of God and two stones in the Ark (woman), to form the " Three-in-one " God, creator of all life. Male in female.

The d'om or dome of the church is simply the "place of the womb," the architecture representing the rounded belly of the "woman" (the man who has the womb), and the "Ark of the Covenant" and Tabernacle were the same symbol, and the Tabernacle was lined with dolphin's skins (delphys, womb) to indicate its symbolic nature. [This is treated fully in my "Christianity" and "Sex Symbolism in Religion."]. So much for the "ineffable" name. We will now consider the host of names derived from the tsur, phallus, or "rock that begat thee," of the Hebrew (really Roman) Scriptures. [For full details of this, see my "Sex Symbolism," Vol. II, "The Romance of the Hebrew Tabernacle."]

In archaic languages, vowels were seldom evolved till long after the "signs" which stood for "things," had been evolved; and the Hebrew, an artificial language, which the Roman Masoretes evolved at Galilee, was practically of consonantal construction. But vowels were found to be absolutely necessary as the work of evolving a sacred book proceeded, and the vowels were made of groups of dots and crosses, and other simple conventional signs added to the skeleton words of consonants.

It is said that a brazen serpent was raised by

Moses for worship (Numb. XXI, 8–9), and this earliest idol, worshipped by the Hebrews, was made into their first letter Al-eph, "god-serpent," written

FIG. 39.—Origin of the Aleph, our A.

א, a rod or phallus caressed by a serpent, and the list of letters was called the alpha-bet, "god-serpent-house," as only by learning to read could scholars (very rare then) enter into the secrets of the priests of the serpent religion, and become members of the fraternity.

The serpent is the most ubiquitous symbol of the life-giving phallus, having been worshipped in every warm climate from Mexico and Central America to Cambodia and Siam, right through Asia and Europe, and having the greatest temples ever erected. The cobra is the chief element on the crown of the Pharaohs of Egypt, showing that they got their religion from India, as the cobra is a purely Indian reptile. India is indeed the "mother of religions," as we shall see. The Hebrews had also Saraphs or Seraphs (Seraphim), serpent columns, from tsur, "the rock that begat thee" (derived like Sarah), or plural Seraphim and Teraphim (Sarah and her father Terah),

and we find Rachel stealing her father's idols, Teraphim (tsur aphim, rock serpents), and sitting on them, and making an excuse to her father for not rising, " I cannot rise before thee ; for the custom of women is upon me " (Gen. XXXI, 35). See how these scribes delight in all phallic tales, but we need not wonder, as all priests were keepers of the " Holy Women "—brothel keepers, with women " consecrated " to prostitution.

These Seraphim were identical with the brazen serpent raised by Moses to cure the syphilis-smitten Hebrews. Even the pole on which serpents were raised is like Solomon's " banner " over his loved one (his " nisi "), a purely phallic word. But Nachash means " serpent," " brazen " and " shameful," and we talk of a " brazen hussie," just as the Romans did, and as they made their great creation (the Hebrews) do.

But as vowels were never written in the beginnings of languages, so all words were recognised by their consonants, and vowel sounds varied as they do now, as may be proved in Britain, as a Cornish miner would not easily understand a Northumberland miner, nor either of them understand a Scottish workman in speech, although they may all read the same newspapers.

The Flood story is also told phallically, but the

Romans introduced many phrases to muddle the story, especially as to beginning and ending, but there are two dates, one the final shutting up of the Ark, and the other its opening, and the time between the two is 284 days, the period of woman's gestation. The Bible says (Genesis VII, 11): " In the six hundredth year of Noah's life, in the second month, the seventeenth day of the month, the same day were all the fountains of the deep broken up, and the windows of heaven were opened." This is a clear final statement that the great Flood had really begun.

Then in Gen. VIII, 13, " And it came to pass in the six hundred and first year, in the first month, the first day of the month, the waters were dried up from off the earth; and Noah removed the covering of the Ark and looked, and, behold, the face of the earth was dry." Life then issued from the Ark (woman). This makes a period of 284 days, the exact period of woman's gestation. The Flood story was extant in the East long before the Romans composed our Bible, but they gave it a practical turn in making a true new birth by particularising the period of gestation. In their moments of elation, however, they get carried away, as when Rebekah is to be " mother of thousands of millions " (Gen. XXIV, 60).

JEHOVAH

IHOH, IHUH or IHVH

Having given my readers some idea of the methods by which Rome built up the history of an imaginary nation, created a language and religious symbols founded on phallic or "life-creative" words and letters, but carefully replacing the signs used by all nations—"dagger and ring," "rod and almond," "Moses's rod of god and two stones," in the female "ark," and so on, by the Roman letters I, O, U, V, and H in some signs, we will now consider their sacred names. These letters, I for the male organ, the Hindoo pala, or pillar, O for the female "door of life," equally expressed by U and V, while H was the "breathing" or "breath-of-life" letter. The O was also symbolised as the "almond," as in Jeremiah I, 11, when IHOH asks Jeremiah, "What seest thou?" and he replied, "I see 'rod and almond,'" not "a rod of an almond tree," as it is stupidly or dishonestly translated. We remember also that

Aaron's rod, which was *not* a tree, brought forth almonds, to form a bi-sexual sacred creative symbol (Numb. XVII, 8), so "rod and almond" are the male and female sex organs, the true "life producers" or "god," or, at least, an old universally-used symbol of the creative god.

IU, the "rod and almond," were the Roman symbols used to construct their Father God IUpiter (or pater), pronounced Yupiter, not "(Dzh)U-piter," as our J makes it. All the J's in our Bible should be I's, as in Latin, or Y's, and in all Eastern, and also continental countries, we stand alone, we Saxons, wherever the otherwise noble English language is spoken, in this barbarism imposed upon us, as all "letters" were, by the clerics or clerks of the Church, for what I believe to be a very sinister purpose—to disguise a great religious fraud.

Or perhaps our clerics were so ignorant as to mistake the German I (of Luther's Bible), which has a crook like our J, and so fell into an error which has hindered English scholarship for all these centuries. All I's in the Bible-names (printed as J), should be pronounced as Ee or Y, and the well-known name Joseph should be Yoseph, as it is now spelt by novel writers treating of their favourite desert Arab "Sheiks," and Levi, which we pronounce " Leave-eye," should have its " e " pronounced as in " left," or as the " ea " and " e " in heaven and its i as double e, as in feet. So the prophet's name Levi, which we mispronounce as " Leeveye," should be vocalised as Levee. With these explanations we may now get on with our Bible studies, and return to the Roman gods. I have dealt with Yupiter or Yove (which we call Dzhupiter and Dzhoav), which name means the double-sexed or creative father. We now come to his wife or consort, IUNO, whom we call Juno, properly pronounced Yuno, or You Know. Here again the male and female " reproductive pair " IU are coupled with the female symbol NO, making the name mean the double-sexed or creative mother, O emphasising the female nature ; O, being the ring of Yima, or the door of life, is often coupled with M and N to make a pronounceable word. The M is truly feminine, as it is the first sound a baby emits as it opens its mouth to cry for milk, " Ma," and that syllable was the name of the first Queen of Heaven, and is adopted as " Mammalia," milk-producing animals, etc., into scientific English. But M and N are the only letters formed by nasal breathing, the M by closing the lips and the N by closing the palatal passage by the tongue, and making the breath

issue by the nose, so N is often used as a feminine
terminal in place of the more obvious female M.
We have also " Una," a very feminine figure, but
being represented as a creative god by being seated
on the strongly male lion. The Hindoo pair
shown here has mother and child seated on the

FIG. 41.—An Indian Una.

lion, but also the skull at her middle, showing
deadly consequence of the " holy " woman's life.
There is another goddess, Umma (or Uma), a
variant of Una, and these minor celestial beings
show the feminine signification of U, M, N, and A.
Una's name begins with the feminine U, which is

FIG. 49. UNA ON HER LION WITH THE EROTIC APPLE.

emphasised by adding a second female term, Na, making her almost identical with Iuno (Juno), but she has no male element I in her name, so she is not a " creative " or double-sexed goddess by herself, but with the lion she makes the creative pair. Egyptian, Hindoo, and Chinese religions had also the nude maid on the lion's back.

There is another variant of Umma, the M, female sign, twice repeated. In Minerva we have a quadruple name ; Min is the ithypallic god of Egypt and Crete (the Minoans, Min-O-ans), and Er is El, Jacob's god, and V and A are each a female sign.

But Erva means the god of the " four quarters," or universal god, so the ithyphallic god is god of all knowledge, and knowledge is always phallic : " Adam knew his wife Eve," or David on his death-bed, when he " knew not " the beautiful Shunammite damsel they put in bed beside him " that my lord may get heat." Erva is AlBa, inverted Baal, god of prostitution. The Hindoos have also a " Na " termination in their god's name, Christna, male-female creative god, on whom we found our Christ (more correctly Christos). The Romans added the female Os to the Christ instead of the female Na, to make a difference between the Indian god and its Roman copy.

K

But Na and Os are equally female particles. Our parsons always try to cover up "dangerous" names. They make us say Kreist for Christ (Kreest), but we don't say Kreistian for Christian; so Christna and our Christos are identical in signification and as individuals.

Lastly, there is the grammatical A, or Ah, used in Latin to indicate a grammatically feminine word, and used in Bible words quite frequently, as in Sarah, as I shall presently explain.

But the Romans decided that such letters were too clearly expressive of the sex idea, so they decided to found their official Bible on letters which revealed nothing to the eye, as I have shown on p. 14 earlier in this book.

On these symbolisms they constructed a language derived in great part from Chaldean and Arabic roots, but constructed in such a complicated manner as to be useless for conversation, and it was "never spoken" (*Encyc. Bib.*, "unvocalised," col. 3,272). In fact, the Romans created Hebrew as a sacred language, in imitation of the Zend of Persia, a secret ecclesiastical language for the priests alone. That it was never spoken or written by the Jews or Hebrews in Palestine is shown by the fact that there is not a scrap of Hebrew or any other language or script other than cuneiform and Egyptian hierogly-phics in all Palestine, says Naville, writing on the " Discovery of the Book of the Law " ; so not one word of Hebrew existed in Palestine up till the Roman possession, nor was it known till the Bible was produced many centuries later. The name Palestine was a creation of the Romans, as was Philistine, both names being from the Hindoo " pala," the male organ, with the Eastern word " stan " for land—the land of " pala " worship ; Philistine, being the same word, but derived from the Greek corruptions of pala to philis, and stan to stine. The Greeks were great corrupters of languages. But the corruptions suited the Romans, giving two names from pala. The Romans took in hand the creation of an old literature with archaic gods, like Job's very rude Al Shadai, the micturator. Iove tells Job that the Behemoth is " chief of the ways of God." The " chief of the ways " of all gods is " creative " power, and so Job's Behemoth was identical in symbolic meaning with the Min, or the Dad of Egypt ; in fact, Job uses the word El for god, and Jacob declares that the stone phallus he erected was El, the god of Israel. But Job introduces the idea of birth in his simile, " surely the mountains bring forth food for him," and again,

" where all the beasts of the field *play*." But *play* is not the English meaning of the original. The reader will find it in the story of Isaac and Abimelech, when Abimelech caught Isaac " sporting " or " playing " with Rebekah, which " playing " proved to Abimelech that Rebekah was Isaac's wife—not his sister ; or in Exodus XXII, with the Israelites "leaping and playing" before

FIG. 42.—THE BEHEMOTH CREATING LIFE.
Female figure broken.

the golden calf, " for Aaron had made them naked unto their shame," or David " leaping and dancing " before the Ark, when his wife, with married dignity, sarcastically said, " How glorious was the King of Israel to-day, who uncovered himself to-day, in the eyes of the handmaidens of his servants, as one of the vain fellows shame-

lessly uncovereth himself " (2 Samuel VI, 20).
This " leaping and dancing " is given in the great
Hebrew lexicons as a " rapid to and fro motion
of his piercer." How shamelessly literal were
these Roman composers of our Bible ! To return
to the Behemoth, or Leviathan, this animal or
god is described as exactly the same as Iové is
described by David in 2 Sam., XXII, 9, where he is
praising IHOH (the " Lord ") for delivering him
from Saul—" There went up a smoke out of his
nostrils, and fire out of his mouth devoured; coals
were kindled by it," while he (IHOH) describes
himself again to Job as the Leviathan. " Out of
his nostrils a light doth shine . . . out of
his mouth go burning lamps, and sparks of fire
leap out. Out of his nostrils goeth smoke. His
breath kindleth coals, and a flame goeth out of his
mouth."

There is a great deal of this sort of " fearsome
dragon " writing in the Bible, no doubt to include
the fables of many tribes, but they nearly always
accompany some phallic story or parable, and that
is the case with Job's Behemoth and Leviathan,
both phallic creators. The name is not very
clear, as its only proposed " root " is in the
Arabic " to be dumb," a phrase having nothing
to do with the story, which is intensely phallic;

in fact, Job tells us that this Behemoth (a plural word) is "chief of the ways of God," that is "creation of life," and he tells us that "his strength is in his loins," and that "he moveth or erecteth his 'tail' like a cedar" (phallus or tree stem) "and the sinews of his stones are wrapped together with strength," then "creation" begins.

Nearly all words beginning with B are intensely phallic, as is Bamoth or Behemoth.

My reason for calling attention to the phallic nature of the Behemoth story is to show the phallic character of the name, and of the root word from which it comes, as it is the root of many important Bible words, all based in the letter B.

The worship of Baal as a defection from IHOH is constantly condemned in the Old Testament story. Now Baal is derived from Baah, to "make to swell" or to "swell out," or to "seek," a description of erect "seeking" phallus, full of "desire" (like Min of Egypt), as in Bum, Bom, Bam, Bamah, Bamoth, Behemoth, etc. (all phallic), from the root Ba, making, with Al, the most phallic god Baal, the lewd god, ithyphallic, like Osiris or Min of Egypt, and Basar, the loathsome, "stinking god," as we may learn from any good lexicon. Again, the root word Bom or Bum means a "high place" or pulpit (pul = pala, and pit, the "yoni," two sexes in coition). Pit in Isaiah III, 17, "make naked the secret parts (pittoth) of the daughters of Israel."

The scribes are constantly railing against the "high places," and we find young maidens "going up" to draw water at these "high places" (1 Samuel IX, 11). This is a phallic passage. The mention of young maidens at a "high place," "drawing water," means sexual intercourse at a priests' brothel. There was a great feast—"Hag"—going on with these maidens, and all great feasts in savage nations mean rich food and wine and women.

Baal Bamoth means the "stinking god of the Pulpits," and Pulpit is the two sex organs combined.

The verse refers to a feast (Hag) such as I have described (see the Uapés on the Amazon, or the Romans), but which existed and still exists all over the world among savages. (p. 41.)

We find many cases of children's rhymes drawn from solemn religious rites. Jack and Jill going up the hill for "water," and both being damaged often happened when syphilis broke out. The priests who wrote our Bible were terribly cynical.

These "consecrated" or "dedicated" women

were simply the priests' slaves, as on their prostitution depended the whole revenue of the temples on which the priests lived. "Consecration," like dedication, simply means the declaration that any person or thing is "devoted" or condemned to any service, "however vile," demanded by the priests. Of course, the "service" was quite honourable at that time, and absolutely necessary to obtain funds to maintain the priests and the temples. In those rude times Emperors visited the sacred prostitutes. But the promiscuity of the system caused terrible epidemics of syphilis. That is why the new Hindoo or Greek son of god, Jesus, or IesU, goes about with Mary Magdalene (Mary of the Almond) as his constant companion, while rudely repelling his mother, "woman, what have I to do with thee," and despising Mary's hard-working, tidy, moral sister, Martha. So common was incest with their mothers and sisters amongst the ancient and mediæval priesthood, that laws had to be enacted again and again, making such cohabitation a crime ; and even then it was common, but no one cared to prosecute the holy father, just as when priests in Ireland are prone to a "drop too much," the people turn their "blind eye" towards his conduct or condition. The group of letters IHOH (יהוה in Hebrew), which we call Jehovah, is the same as another symbol of eternal life, or the endless reproduction of life, the famous " Ark of the Covenant," which contained the rod of God, I, and his two breath-of-life stones, HH, in the female Ark (all ships or arks are female), represented by the letter O, Yima's " ring " for creating life, or the womb or woman (the man who has the womb), making IHOH.   These letters formed the supreme emblem of the most holy god, and it was death to attempt to pronounce the name, or to touch the Ark. Uzzah (2 Sam. VI, 6–8) was struck dead for even putting forth his hand to steady the Ark when he innocently thought that it might fall from the swaying of the wagon conveying it.   Yet this famous Ark of God was only one of the little systems which " have their day and cease to be" when Jeremiah (pronounced Yeremyah) III, 16, orders that "they shall say no more, the Ark of the Covenant of the Lord, neither shall it come to mind, neither shall they remember it, neither shall they visit it, neither shall it be done any more." The Hebrew Ark is called " Aron," and is itself double-sexed or creative.   Ar is Al (as L and R are identical in old languages), a male god, and " on " is feminine, like " om," womb, a creative pair, like the monstrance and pyx.

That the two stones, symbolised by the cross-piece on the phallic pillar forming our cross, are essential to life or life-production, and a sign of life after death, is made clear by the discovery by the late Dr. Angus Smith and myself when, opening some old cromlechs or burial mounds near Oban quite 50 years ago, we found in several graves a cavity over the heads of the skeletons containing two small oval stones of white quartz such as are found plentifully on most pebbly beaches. Here were the two breath-of-life emblems, similar to Moses's two stones in the Ark, in use as a resurrection symbol long before the Christian era.

The Egyptians, through whom many of these ideas came, from their knowledge of the anatomy of the human body owing to their custom of embalming, and from the existence of Eunuchs, no doubt knew of another pair of Eduth (or witnesses or stones, from " testimony "), the ovaries, so the two H's may have also symbolised the female " origins of life " equally with the male. The ovaries are quite a sacred emblem, and we have, in London, a church hitherto called " Saint Mary of the Ovaries," which too phallic name has just (1924) been changed to " Southwark Cathedral." The Church is becoming shy of this all-

too-naked phallic language, which, in the Old
Testament, is undermining the people's " faith "
in the foreign " Hebrew " religion forced on us by
the Romans.

But the priest was seldom content with a
symbolic or cryptic phrase meaning only one
thing, he loved to make a " letter combination "
which was equally applicable to several ideas, so
his HOH, the " breath-of-life " letters on each side
of O, the woman, can be spelt in Greek as Eve
(H and E being the same letter in Greek).   Eve
was therefore a goddess (symbolically at least).
This four-letter holy name, the " tetragrammaton," was so holy that anyone attempting to
pronounce the name or inquiring into its meaning
was punished with death, so it was parallel with
the monstrance and pyx and the Ark.   I think
they have now dropped out of all the forms of
Christianity as " practical propositions."   The
Hindoo word " pala " has penetrated the English
language, and produced numerous offspring.   We
have sacred words such as " pall," a cloth placed
over a dead person to insure re-birth, " palace,"
the place where the " mace," king, and other
highly sacred things or people dwell in Rome on
the " Palatine " Hill (Palatine is Palestine, Philistine, etc.).   Palladium, Palatinate, one ruling like

a king, the phallus being a universal emblem of kings [O King! live for ever]. "Pala" for the individual staves in a "paling," a series of "palas," "within the pale," palenque, a name given to

FIG. 43.—Dead Osris.

Central American Indians who worshipped pillars or palas, Palas the Goddess of Knowledge (Adam knew his wife Eve, "the serpent was wise"), palisade from palus, a stake (also phallus), pallad-

ium, the phallus god, and so on. Pala became
phallos by Greek corruption, then phallus in Latin,
so we call all things relating to the male organ
" phallic." The Roman race was very highly
phallic, and so is the Bible they produced. In
Egypt, instead of a pall or eternal-life cloak being
spread over the dead Osiris, his pala was always
rendered " ithyphallic," to show his lively condition as a god-like Min, although his earthly
body was dead. In Fig. 43 the maidens are tearing their hair and chafing Osiris's sex member
to keep his soul alive (the member being here
omitted). Egypt and India are full of such figures
as this, which, of course, I cannot reproduce in full,
but the literal way they were represented may be
shown by a page of one of the best-known lexicons
on hieroglyphics, which always shows the male
organ active (p. 64). Our translators mis-translate
many Bible passages to avoid these expressions.

The names Palestine and Philistine are simply
compositions of the Hindoo Pala with " Stan," land,
meaning lands of the worship of the Phallus (male
god) and of Philis (love, or female god), like Hindu-
stan, Afganistan or Baluchistan, lands of the
Hindus, Afgans and Baluchis (palakis.)

We therefore inherit, or adopt a " shameful "
religion, as the Oxford professors well know.

NEW TESTAMENT NAMES

Let us take the principal name in the New Testament in the original Greek, Iesu Christos [Yaisoo Kreestos], whom we erroneously call Jesus Christ, in fact we say Jesus the Christ, Christ being the more ancient and authoritative name or title. He is also hailed by us as the " Saviour," which is likewise a very old term applied to gods and men, for instance in the case of Ptolemy " Soter," who was termed Soter, " Saviour," 300 years before the supernatural " God in the flesh," Jesus, was supposed to appear on this earth. " Saviours " were plentiful in all countries where a supernatural religion existed, and we have had a recent example in the Greek Venizelos, who was lately hailed as the " Saviour " of the Greeks, who declared that his " advent " had been long foretold.

I gave in my Christianity a list of 26 Messiahs or Saviours, " Messiah " being " Son of Iah," or Jah, and Iah, a double-sexed god, I, masculine pillar, and Ah, feminine particle, used in Bible names such as Isaiah, pronounced Eesa-yah, and not Eye-say-yah, as we ignorantly pronounce it. Messiah, Mess-yah, has no derivation from any word meaning " anointed," as some assert, Mes-Iah simply means Son of Iah, short for Jehovah in Old Testament names. Nor does Christ arise from chrio, " to anoint," as others assert. Christ is the " shining one," the sun. We must not forget that in the original Bible there is no Christ, it is always Christos (pronounced Kreestos) in Greek, and Christus in Latin. Christ is our English corruption and completely mispronounced.

The two names Christos and Christna have identical symbolic meaning, the Na and Os being the feminine symbols for phallic imagery in India and Greece. Christna, like Christos, was a Sun-God.

The Hindoo " Na " was translated into OS in Greek, O being the chief female symbol and S constantly used in female words such as sister, sistrum, isis, etc., and the two letters meaning " mouth " in Latin.

Christna was undoubtedly the Hindoo Sun-God, and as the IesU was called *The Christ*, he was simply a copy of the Hindoo god modernised to Roman opinion and with a Roman symbolism. Now our Christ is a Sun-God born at the New Year, our Christmas (which is even nearer to the real

New Year (22nd December) than is our nominal
" New Year's Day "), passes over, or " crosses "
over by " making a crossing," the true meaning
of crucifixion, at the Spring Equinox, to the
salvation of mankind from the certain death of
perpetual winter.

Crucifixion means " to make a crossing," not " to
be fixed on a cross." Christos and Christna are both
transfigured with a " shining light," the sun. All
heavenly saviours were those who made a crossing
to save mankind from death by perpetual winter.
All Saviours were Suns. The " crossing " was, of
course, over the Equator at the Spring equinox,
from the Southern to the Northern hemisphere,
" bringing," in popular language, " summer "
or " Salvation from a wintry death."

But besides these similarities, the adjoining list
(pp. 147–149) will show that our Christos is a
slavish copy of Christna, as I show in the adjoining
list of identical incidents which I place here for
ready reference. (I give a detailed list with
references later in this book.) Christna lived 800
years before Christos, and the Christian Saviour's
name should be pronounced Yaisu Kreestos.

IDENTICAL INCIDENTS (CHRIST AND CHRISTNA)

(1) Born of a chaste woman
(2) Real father, Spirit of God
(3) Additional father
(4) Of royal descent
(5) Contradictory genealogies
(6) Deity in human form
(7) Angels hail the virgin
(8) Birth announced by a star
(9) Virgin names alike (Mary and Maya)
(10) Miraculous father
(11) Celestial music at birth
(12) Born in a cave, or stable
(13) Cave filled with light
(14) Angels sing at night
(15) Spoke immediately on birth
(16) Adored by shepherds (men who depend on the sun)
(17) Magi guided by star
(18) Earthly father carpenter (maker, creator)
(19) Jewels and ointment given by Magi
(20) Born poor, but of royal descent
(21) Father away, paying taxes
(22) Shown in a manger
(23) Mother on a journey, at an inn
(24) Preceded by a forerunner
(25) Rulers Kanza and Herod
(26) Stayed at Maturea,* India

* Maturea is not in Egypt.

(27) Very learned when young
(28) Chosen king by boy companions
(29) Son of father's old age
(30) Father warned of attempt to kill babe
(31) Both babes taken to Maturea,* India
(32) Father and mother fled
(33) Babes killed, Christ and Christna saved
(34) King slays forerunner
(35) Babes' life preserved
†(36) Made " fish ponds " (pisces)
†(37) Jesus slew boy who broke ponds
(38) Miracles (blind, lame, sick, etc., all kinds same for both)
(39) Beginning of religious life, fasted
(40) Devil offered kingdom of the world
(41) Reproved Satan
(42) Anointed by a poor woman
(43) Twelve Apostles (sun and twelve months)
†(44) Chose two fishers, Simon and Andrew, pisces
†(45) Two more fishers, James and John
†(46) Two ships
†(47) Chose Simon, James and John (fishers)
†(48) Miraculous draft of fishes
†(49) Fishers as Apostles
†(50) Feeds 5,000
†(51) Tribute money from fishes' mouth
†(52) Fed 4,000 with 7 loaves and a few small fishes (Christ, only sun, entered fish sign)
(53) Bruising head of serpent
(54) Transfigured before Disciples
(55) Meekest and mildest of men
(56) Alpha and Omega
(57) Crucified marks on hands and side

* Maturea is not in Egypt.

(58) Crucified, sun dark, consoled thief
(59) Pierced
(60) Descended into Hell
(61) Rose from the dead
(62) Ascended into Heaven
(63) Many saw him ascend
(64) Will return on horse, stars will fall out of the sky
(65) Judge on the last day
(66) Beloved Disciple, John, Arjuna (the John)
(67) Creator of all things
(68) Transfigured with shining light
(69) Second person in the Trinity
†(70) After resurrection eats *fish* ⎫ Christ
†(71) After resurrection miraculous draft of fishes ⎭ only
(72) Light of the world
(73) True Vine-Sun (Jesus was a Sun-God)
(74) " Jesus " Christ was IesU, the ⎫ IU Roman
Indo-European god ⎭ ES Hindoo
(75) and " Christ," the Eastern Sun-God Christna
(76) Combined by Romans as one god
(77) To consolidate the empire, while
†(78) Sun passed into pisces, hence fishermen and fishes

Roman   Jesus is IesU ; IU Roman is double-sex,
| God | a creative god, and ES Hindoo for " Flesh,"
I es U   making the " God in the Flesh " of the Gospel.
| | † These apply to Christ, not to Christna, as
Hindoo   Christ was born when the sun was in
Flesh   " Pisces," hence " Fish " miracles.

The lives of the two gods are identical except where their astronomical lives differ, Christna being 800 years earlier than Christos, so our Christos must be the copy and Christna the original. Our Christos or Christus was created in celebration of the passing of the sun from the constellation of the Ram or Lamb at the Spring equinox (date of birth of all Saviours) into the constellation of the Fishes, hence all the fish miracles and fishermen Apostles of the Christ, and fishing boats. The sign of Pisces is a pair of fishes, and Jesus's fisher Apostles and fish miracles are also in pairs, two fishermen twice repeated, two fishing boats, two little fishes twice repeated. He walks on the water and again eats fish with his Apostles *after resurrection*, before he " ascends " to produce summer and says " do this in remembrance of me." So the " fishes " sign was to become a Sacrament, but fish is decidedly a disagreeable article, so this sign soon dropped out ; but a pair of fishes were cut on tombstones for three or four hundred years after the Christ legend was introduced. The cross, a very old symbol to represent the equinoctial crossing, and the phallus, or a sex religion, was finally adopted as the Christian sign. When we come to attempt to penetrate the veil of false history thrown over Palestine before the

arrival of the Romans, but written in our Bible as
the actual ancient history by the official Roman
scribes or priests, we find that it was such a barren,
useless land that it, like parts of the vast Arabia,
had no history except that of a field of battle
between invading northern hordes and Egyptian
defenders of their rich, fertile lands, the Nile being
one of the most famous sources of fertility in the
eastern world, and always coveted by the inhabitants of lands with severe winters.   The ruins of
Egyptian palaces and barracks for soldiers right
up to Beisan, the gateway to Tyre, prove that
Palestine had a long history as an Egyptian province, no doubt open to attack from the north by
the hardy, blood-thirsty Ninevites and Babylonians, always with the war-lust in their blood.
They gloried in brute strength, as is witnessed
in their sculpture—their men with mighty muscles
realistically carved, and always in battles against
man and beast, or driving trussed-up, tortured
captives, for slaughter or slavery, or lashing slaves
to urge them to greater efforts in building, while
their women were full-breasted, stocky females,
fit mates for such " brute-force " men.

Ptolemy Soter was fighting in Palestine 300 years
B.C., but it had no such name then, and its
possession was a " give and take " game between

the northern races such as the Hittites and the southerns, Egypt or Arabia—but it was always a land of no consequence except as a barrier held by Egypt to prevent the hungry northern tribes wishing to conquer the rich Egypt. There was always " corn in Egypt." It was, of course, the only stepping-stone from north to south or *vice versa* from Egypt to Asia.

But before our history begins it was held long enough, probably for several hundreds or even thousands of years, to enable the Egyptians to establish great palaces and barracks, the ruins of which have just been discovered, by the excavators from Philadelphia University, and which are only now being examined on both sides of the Jordan and up to Beisan, the northern gateway to the port of Tyre. So " Solomon and all his glory " were a pure creation of the imagination, or perhaps a dim shadow of the actual palaces of the Egyptians—conjured into life by the " romance " writers of the Old Testament. Artificial stories are well-named " romances," as the Romans were the prime creators of fictitious history. Of course, the hundreds of millions of pounds' value of gold in the Temple was stretching the imagination a bit too far. In any case, such palaces as befitted governors and generals *did* exist prior to the

Roman conquest of Egypt, when the Egyptian possessions fell into Roman hands and were, no doubt, promptly occupied by Roman soldiers, unless they were destroyed during some of the outbreaks of war always taking place. Great conquests had already been made far East, and Rome planned to extend her empire and to consolidate it, in fact, dreamed of world-conquest. But in these days of scant roads and slow communication and a terribly extended Empire, Rome found that it was extremely difficult to hold these conquests, as it took more soldiers to hold them in subjection than it did to conquer them, as the conquests were done one by one in detail, while insurrections broke out simultaneously in lands far distant. *It was under pressure of these conditions, with her empire crumbling, that Rome conceived the idea of a universal religion, giving a power above Kings to the agents of the Holy Father in Rome.* They decided to construct their great Book as quietly as possible and announce it as the true " Word of God," and, by appointing Cardinals, Archbishops, and Bishops everywhere, they hoped to create a power above kings, and impose Rome's will on the conquered peoples, aided by a terrible and secret power—the confessional—greater than that of arms, and the

Bishop who crowned any king could, on his disobeying Rome's mandate, depose him from his high position. The secret curse of Rome made cowards of all peoples, so a disobedient monarch had difficulty in gaining support, all were afraid of this great secret mysterious organisation, whose mandates were obeyed to the uttermost confines of the Empire. But we are not interested in the political side of the Roman world revolution, so, to return to our text, the Roman religion.

The control of the temple brothels gave Rome immense local power. As the tide of biblical criticism rose from a few weak criticisms (the authors of which were ostracised by staunch churchmen) and grew into a broad stream which could no longer be treated as something to be frowned down, the Church scholars at Oxford conceived the idea of having all the learning already accumulated collected into a great encyclopædia. The scholars who had made timid nibblings at the great questions, such as miracles, or the divinity of the Christ, felt that the protection of a great work which would include all the most advanced studies of men whose discoveries were so startling and yet so authentic that their publication could not be prevented by the frowns of the Church, would enable them to step forward

and give the world the benefit of their life-long
investigations. It was thought by many that
this would strengthen the Church, as it would cut
away doubtful dicta and let the truth shine out.
Well, many of us were disappointed, and in many
cases the mountain and mouse fable was aptly
illustrated. But others, myself included, saw that
enough had been proved by these writers to make
a considerable breach in the Orthodox Church's
defences, so I was emboldened to put notes I had
accumulated during forty years' reading into rough
book form, and I published my " Christianity, the
Sources of its Teaching and Symbolism," in 1913.
I had been pretty reticent in that book, and, as
I saw that no one had been greatly offended, I
published during the War six little books with
various titles, all studies from different points
of view, such as " The Gods of the Hebrew
Bible," " The Queen of Heaven," " The Seven
Stories of Creation," and so on, latterly grouping
them all together under the title of " Sex Symbolism in Religion," and so began to get a small
audience. I then decided to give a short account
of some of my discoveries of what is under the
covers of the Christian Bible, hence the present
work. As my other works are in all the principal
University and municipal libraries, and so are

available to readers, I do not repeat in the present volume all I have detailed in the others, but I think I have stated sufficient here to make this volume a complete study in itself. I would add that I cannot relate all my discoveries in an open book, as much of the text is too grossly indecent for translation of the special tales used by the Masoretes, written to introduce the peoples of Europe and Asia to the immoral teachings of their brothel-keeping clergy.

The name Iesu, our Jesus, is a curious combination of Roman and Indian symbolism. The IU are, of course, frankly Roman, as in their " IUpiter " or " IUno," our Jupiter and Juno. But the " es " has a very different origin. The great god of India had a long titular name, and was double-sexed, like IHOH and IesU. He was called Ardha-Nari Eswara, the first half of the compound name, Ardha-Nari, meaning half male and half female, like IU, or like " Hermaphroditic " and " Omphallic " (compounds of Mercury and Venus, and of their equivalents, womb and phallus), or creative gods. The second half of his name, Eswara, means the " ward " or guardian of the " flesh "—it may mean of " all flesh," or of the flesh of his nakedness, *i.e.*, the " phallus," as the continuer of life, or producer of life to

eternity.   This is the idea of saviour of humanity
so that life shall not fail, as when at the Flood the
gods (plural Elohim) say, " The end of all flesh is
before me " [literally the " measure " of all flesh].
The whole point of the New Testament story is
the descent of a god to earth and embodying
himself in a fleshly or human form, and we find the
phrase " God sending his son in likeness of sinful
flesh " (the " Es " of India), Romans VIII, 3 (1),
and Romans, I, 3, says " his son, Jesus Christ our
Lord, made of the seed of David according to
the *flesh* " (2), and in Romans, IX, 5, " as concern-
ing the *flesh* Christ came " (3), also in the following
verses :—(See p. 47, and foot of p. 149.)

Romans, VIII, 1, " In Christ Jesus, who walk
not after the *flesh* " (4).

2 Corinthians, IV, 11, " That the life also of
Jesus might be made manifest in our mortal
flesh " (5).

2 Corinthians, IV, 16, " We have known Christ
after the *flesh* " (6).

Acts, II, 31, Resurrection of Christ, " Neither
did his *flesh* suffer corruption " (7).

1 Timothy, III, 16, " God was manifest in the
flesh " (8).

1 Peter, IV, 1, " Christ suffered for us in the
flesh " (9).

I John, IV, 2, " Jesus Christ is come in the *flesh* " (10).

Galatians, V, 24, " And they that are Christ's having crucified the *flesh* " (11).

Philippians, III, 3, " Rejoice in Jesus Christ and have no confidence in the *flesh* " (12).

Here we have an indication of sun-worship. There are 12 months in the sun's year, 12 Apostles, and we have 12 declarations of the combination of IU, or the Roman god IUpiter, with Es, the Hindee for " flesh," and many other " 12 " symbols. The gods of all intelligent nations were founded on sun-worship, as without the sun universal death would reign. So the sun is the Saviour, and we have several indications of this cult in the New Testament story, as well as in the Old Testament, as in Exodus, XXIV, 17, " and the sight of the glory of the Lord (IHOH) was like a devouring fire on the top of the mount, in the eyes of the Children of Israel," and verse 10, " and they saw the God of Israel, there was under his feet as it were a paved work of sapphire stones, and as it were the body of heaven in his clearness," a good description of the sun in a blue sky in Arabia. Les U was the " Light of the World " (Sun).

To return to the " God-in-the-flesh " texts.

This is a very important statement repeated

12 times, and coupled with the 12 Apostles, 12
months, and many other twelves, his "sun's"
course in birth, transit, and ascension, as Christna
is equally a sun-god with Christos ; and his life
(800 years before IesU, in fact 1,400 years before.
the Bible came out) is identical with that of our
Christ ; showing that the Romans went to India
to Asoka's teaching (following Siddartha) for the
whole basis of the Christian (Christna) religion.

Even the name Christos or Christus, Greek and
Roman (our " Christ " is a defective word) reveals
the Hindoo origin, as Christna is a male-female
combination, " n " and " a " being both female
signs, as I have shown, while in our Christos or
Christus, the O and U symbolise the female organ,
and the S is a universal indication of the female,
as in isis, isa, isha, for woman, etc., sister, systrum,
etc., all female. Thus the two names equally
denote the god-power of sex creation, Christna
being symbolically identical with Christos or
Christus. We English cut off the " us " and os,"
and, *if we do so with the Indian " na," we have
identical names, " Christ," in both tongues.* Some
writers spell the Indian god's name with a K to
make a difference, but the European Christ is
spelt in some parts of south-eastern Europe and
in Russia with a K, just as the Germans correctly

spell Jesus Iesu, and call him " Herr Iesu Christi,"
" Mr Jesus Christ," terribly shocking to devout
English ears.

Then we have the whole data of events in the
life of Jesus. Born at Christmas, the sun's birth-
day, or as near as the state of astronomical
knowledge allowed [our New Year is ten days
late], crossed over or crucified at the Spring
equinox, bringing Summer to the salvation of
mankind, because, if the sun did not cross over,
there would be no Summer in the northern
temperate zone, no crops, and universal death
would ensue. Jesus was crucified, "made to
cross," not crucifixed.

He then ascends, produces Summer, or
" salvation " from the death of perpetual winter.

So we have in the Christian religion, as in all
the religions of strong intelligent nations, the
combination of " phallism " and " sun-worship,"
to express the upholding of life by the sex organs
in the body of man on earth and by the sun in the
heavens.

But to return to the Hindoo god, the name
Ardha-Nari means half of each sex (double sex),
and the name IesU contains the IU of IUpiter
and IUno, our Jupiter and Juno, and we have
the IOseph (Joseph) and Iah (Nehemiah, etc.)
of hundreds of names in the Old Testament, male

and female symbols. But, in the case of Jesus, correctly Iesu (Yaisu) and placed between the two letters IU, denoting divinity, we have the Hindoo Es, " flesh," making the symbol of a god appearing as a man or a man's form, " flesh " enveloped in the god-like creative IU, or divine spirit, as IU is double sex or a god. We pity the poor benighted Hindoo or Buddhist praying to a carving in wood or stone which embodies the two sex organs, which, after all, do represent " eternal life," while we (I include Catholics with Protestants) adore the male organ alone (in the Cross), and pray to a detailed description of copulation, IHOH, which we call " Jehovah " or " Lord,' and we make our ordained speakers address us on a divine (god of wine) subject, from a pulpit, a Hebrew description and model of the two sex organs *in coitu*—" pul," the phallus, and " pit," the sex organ of woman, as shown. in Isaiah (Eesa yah), III, 16–17, where he complains : " Because the daughters of Zion are haughty and walk with stretched-out necks, and wanton eyes, walking and mincing as they go, and making a tinkling with their feet. Therefore the Lord (IHOH) will smite with a scab the crown of the head of the daughters of Zion, and the Lord will make naked their secret parts (pittoth, plural of

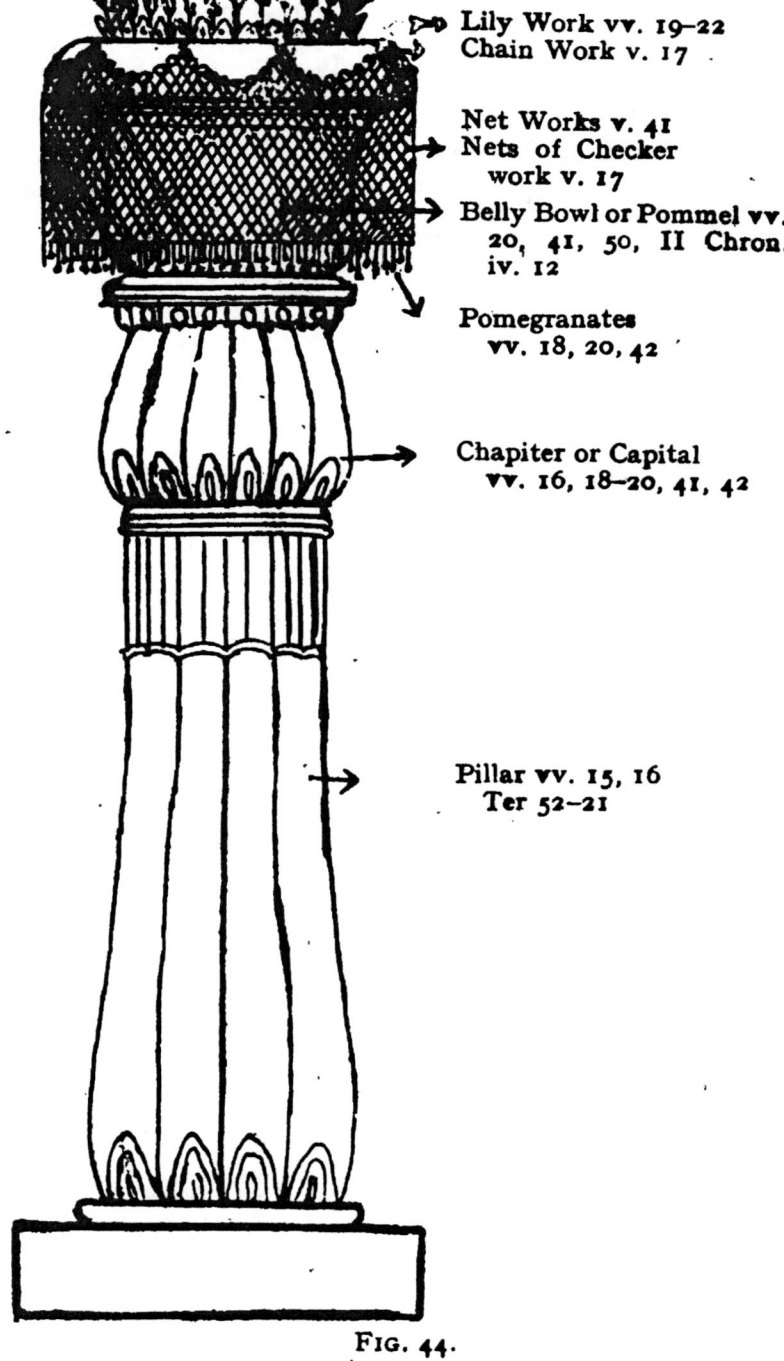

Jakin and Boaz
I Kings VII, 10–14, 20–28

Lily Work vv. 19–22
Chain Work v. 17

Net Works v. 41
Nets of Checker
work v. 17

Belly Bowl or Pommel vv.
20, 41, 50, II Chron.
iv. 12

Pomegranates
vv. 18, 20, 42

Chapiter or Capital
vv. 16, 18–20, 41, 42

Pillar vv. 15, 16
Ter 52–21

FIG. 44.

pit, the female member)." So " pulpit " means
coition, male and female parts in the creative act.
This was clearly illustrated in the detailed description in 1 Kings, VII, 10–14, and 20–28, illustrated here from a sketch in my " Sex Symbolism,"
Vol. I, p. 200. The Egyptians had the same

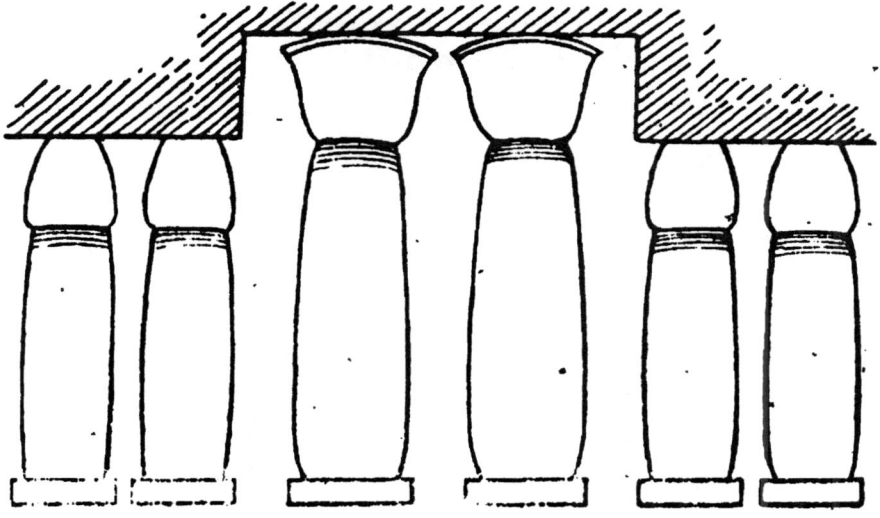

FIG. 45.

Egyptian male pillars right and left, and double-sexed
pillars creating life in the middle. The latter are exactly
the same as those described as Jakin and Boaz in our Bible.

symbolism, but they often put the simple male
column of the circumcised phallus in the outer
work of temple collonades, and gave the double-
sex column a more sacred place like our IHOH
(Jehovah), as shown in this rough sketch (Fig. 45).

M

They also made the double-sexed column of a greater height and importance than the male alone, just as the Romans did in their " Hebrew " scriptures, making IHOH, double-sex, their most sacred name, while IO, mere coition, was freely used in men's names. It would take many volumes to trace the same ideas through all religions; from the most civilised to the most savage, their ideas all ran in the groove of the double-sex production of life. The Hebrew Jakin and Boaz (the ancestor) were the same, more elaborately carried out (Fig. 44). (Fig. on p. 162.)

We call our worshippers together by a double-sexed bell, a name derived from pala, or pul, with a pestle (the Hebrew for the male organ), which we call the tongue, a common phallic symbol when protruded, as in Egyptian sculpture. Bull, the animal representing male strength, is the same word. We have Ephod's " snake and testicles " (or witnesses), cloaks, which are whipped "off and on " the sovereign at coronation, to make him divine, and they anoint him with holy oil called semen in Hebrew (a Latin word for seed) out of a spoon called an ampul (om phalla), double-sexed name, in order to make him " live for ever."

Lastly, our most holy personage, " Jesus Christ," or " IesU the Shining One " (the sun), is equally phallic ; IesU meaning the two sex organs " in the flesh," or eternal life (a god), descending and living " in the flesh " on earth.

We do not officially say Jesus Christ like John Smith, but we say Jesus *the* Christ, as his history is not that of the double-sex creative god, but of a sun-god who came on earth to symbolise the sun's return to save man from winter, and is denoted by Christ-na in India and in the New Testament Christ-os, the shining one—the sun. " I am the light of the world."

In fact, we do not say Jesus Christ, but Jesus *the* Christ [of India] ; Rome was very anxious to propitiate India. The *Encyc. Bib*. tells us of the invention of names of mythical people, such as " names of legendary kings " (col. 3,278), " Mythical patriarchs down to Abraham " (col. 3,275), " impossible statistics as to numbers of the Israelite tribes " (col. 3,275), " Mentions many representatives or chiefs of tribes—some of these personages had no existence " (col. 3,275), and " names invented to fill up gaps " (col. 3,275). The *Encyc. Bib*. is sprinkled with phrases, " fabulous," " mythical," " names coined," " impossible " and " names invented to fill up gaps," a fine character to give as to the truthfulness of the parsons' " Word of God." Verily the reverend professors give their Holy Bible a very bad character, in fact they have slain it, and it only awaits interment.

As to the Genesis X, with its genealogies, the *Encyc. Bib.* says, " *here the fictitious character of the list plainly shows itself.*"   I need not quote more, as all Bible names, except those from other countries, are artificial concoctions, and I have no hesitation in asserting that the whole Bible, Old and, New Testament included, is a gigantic fraud perpetrated on humanity to enslave mankind by the Roman priesthood, and to aid in giving the Romans dominion over the lands they had temporally conquered, but which they could not retain by force of arms, so they tried fraud. Of course, the Oxford professors say as little as their scholarship will allow against the authenticity of the " Word of God," *on which their whole organisation is built*—colleges, libraries of theological logomachy, cathedrals, churches, palaces, rectories, parsonages, etc., all depend on upholding the " Holy Bible," but they say enough in their purely literary lucubrations to condemn their " Word of God " as a vast imposture, a purely political engine which the Romans wrote and used to subjugate the people to the priests' will.

In Egypt, where there were constant processions

with such articles as are illustrated at p. 51, arks with Osiris (generally ithyphallic, to show his unabated sex power even after death, like Jesus. The fable which was supposed to give rise to the worship of the phallus was that Typhon slew Osiris (Cain and Abel), and scattered his body in pieces all over Egypt. Search was made and all parts of the body were found except the phallus. Isis caused a model of the lost phallus to be made, and consecrated it, and so introduced phallic worship, and it became the sacred symbol of Egypt, also, as the god Min (Fig. 38). All pillars in Egypt have a phallic form, some masculine and some double-sexed. The English word pillar is simply the pala of India, the name of the erect male organ. We have also the pole, pale (in paling), pall, and pallus gives pallisade, a " paling " of " phali," and balustrade, corrupted finally to banister. The name of the son was quite different, and plainly announced that he was the god " in earthly form." The name IesU is simply the male and female symbols, I, the pillar, male, and U, the yoni, female, making a god (double-sex, creative), and surrounding or clothing with Es, flesh—the flesh of a man ; or the spirit of God in or on man's body. Of course, the English rendering, Jesus, destroys the obvious meaning conveyed by the real name, IesU or IESU, like IU, pater, the IU standing for a god, being a creative couple.

Here again the Romans went to India for their symbolism. The double-sexed god of India is Ardha-Nari Eswara, " Ardha-Nari " meaning half male and half woman, and " Eswara " means guardian of the phallus, hence upholder of life, also " flesh guardian " or " guardian of all flesh " or of the phallus, as the Hindoo " Es " is used, like our flesh, in " fleshly lusts " of scripture. Thus we see that IesU is a name describing an individual of flesh clothed with the spirit of God, or divinity, to use the ancient Chinese Di particle, as the I and U, male and female, enclose the "Es," flesh, or as our Litany says, " God made flesh for us," as repeated 12 times in the Epistles to indicate the 12 months—as Jesus, or IesU, was a sun-god.

IDENTICAL INCIDENTS IN THE LIVES OF CHRISTNA AND CHRISTOS

Incidents.	Christna.	Christos.
1. Born of a chaste mother	*Vishnu Purana*, p. 502 *History of Hindustan*, V. II, p. 327	Matt., I, 20
2. Real father, Spirit of God	Vishnu descended into Devaki's womb	Luke, I, 27
3. Earthly father or foster father	Nanda (*Asiatic Researches*, I, 259)	Apoc. Gospel of Mary, Ch. VII, Matt. and Luke Joseph
4. Of royal descent	Higgins' *Anacalypta, Asiatic Researches*, I, 259	Matt., I, and Luke, III, 24
5. Muddled genealogy	*Hist. Hind.* II, 310	Generations of Jesus
6. Deity in human form	Sir William Jones' *Asiatic Researches*, I, 279-285	Ditto Christian Creed
7. Angels hail virgin	*Hist. Hind.*, II, 270, 329	Mary Apoc. Gospel, VII
8. Birth announced by star	*Hist. Hind.*, II, 317, 336	Matt., II, 2,
9. Name of virgin	Devaki (goddess)	Mary, goddess after death
10. Miraculous father	Holy Spirit, Vishnu	Holy Spirit, God Jehovah

Incidents.	Christna.	Christos.
11. Birth announced by pleasing sounds from sky	*Vishnu Purana*, p. 502	Luke, II, 13
12. Born in an abject and humiliating state in a cave (inn, farm)	*Hist. Hind.*, II, 311	Cave still shown at Bethlehem. Apos. Gosp., sacred cavern, Farrar's *Life of Christ*, p.38
13. Cave filled with light	Cox, *Aryan Myths*, II, p. 133; Higgins' *Anacal.*, 1–13; *Vishnu Purana*, 502 (Wilson)	Luke, II, 8–15; Shepherds watched flocks by night
14. Angels sang by night	*Vishnu Purana* (Wilson trans.)	Luke, II, 8–15
15. Spoke to his mother immediately on birth	*Hist. Hind.*, II, 311	Infancy, apoc. Gospels
16. Adored by cowherds and shepherds	Higgins' *Anacalypta*, VI, 129, 130	

Incidents.	Christna.	Christos.
17. Magi guided by stars	*Hist. Hind.*, II, 256, 257 Also *Vishnu Purana* Wise men examine "his star"	Infancy Apoc. Gosp. Matt., II, 2 Matt., XIII, 55, **Mark,** VI, 3
18. Earthly father, carpenter	Chas. Morris, *Aryan Sun Myths*	
19. Costly jewels, precious things, given him by Magi or wise men	Sandal wood and perfumes Amberley's *Analyses*, p. 177 Bunsen's *Angel Messiah,* 36	Matt., II, 2
20. Born poor, but of royal descent	*Asiatic Researches,* I, 259 *Hist. Hind.,* II, 310	Matt. and Luke
21. Father away paying taxes	*Vishnu Purana,* V, Ch. III	Luke
22. Shown in a manger	*Asiatic Researches,* I, 259	Luke, II, 7
23. Mother on a journey, at an inn	*Aryan Sun Myths*	Luke, II, 7

Incidents.	Christna.	Christos.
24. Preceded by a forerunner	Rama, *Hist. Hind.*, II, 316	John Baptist
25. Ruler sought forerunner's life	Kanza	Herod
26. Stayed at Maturea or Matura	Mattura is Christna's birthplace	Farrar's *Life of Christ*, Maturea is in India, not Egypt
27. Very learned when young	*Hist. Hind.*, II, 321	Infancy Apoc., Ch. XX, 1–8
28. Chosen king by boy companions	*Hist. Hind.*, II, 321	Inf. Apoc., Ch. XVIII
29. Son of father's old age	*Vishnu Purana*	Gospels
30. Father warned in a dream that king or ruler sought to kill babe	J. C. Semgooly, *Life and Religion of the Hindoos*, p. 134	Matt., II, 13
31. King	Kanza or Kansa	Herod

Incidents.	Christna.	Christos.
32. Father and mother fled	*Asiatic Researches*, I, 233–259	Matt., II, 13
33. Slaughter of innocents so as to include divine babe	Gangooly, p. 134, sculpture in Caves of Elephanta (very ancient)	Matt., II, 16
34. King slays forerunner	*Hist. Hind.*, II, 318 Apoc. Infancy, Higgins' *Anacalpyta*, I, 130	Mark, VI, 14 Matt., II, etc., Gospels
35. Babe's life preserved	Cox, II, 134, *Hist. Hind.*, II, 331	
36. Made fish ponds	No mention of fish	Apoc. Infancy
37. Struck dead boy who broke fish ponds	No mention of fish	Apoc. Infancy
38. Miracles	Raised the dead, cured leper, etc., miracles common to all saviours, but no mention of fishes	Fish miracles and fishermen for Apostles, as Christ was the sun just entering Pisces, the fish constellation

Incidents.	Christna.	Christos.
39. Beginning of religious life, fasted	Moncure D. Conway, *Siamese Life of Buddha*, pp. 44, 172, 173 *Ling. Heng.* of Prof. S. Beal	Matt., IV, 1–11
40. Tempted of the devil, offered empire of the world	Bunsen's *Angel Messiah*, 38–39, Beal, Hardy and others	Matt., IV, Luke, I, 12, Luke, IV,
41. Reproves Satan	Ditto	Ditto
42. Anointed poor woman	*Hist. Hind.*, II, 320	Matt., XXVI, to Mark, XIV, 3, Luke, XII, 37, John, XII, 3
43. Twelve Apostles or Disciples	*Aryan Sun Myths*, 12 months	All Gospels
44. Chose two fishers, Simon and Andrew, for Disciples	No fish or fishers mentioned	Matt., IV, 18

Incidents.	Christna.	Christos.
45. Chose two fishers (James and John)	Ditto	Matt., IV, 21, John, I, 42 (Simon, Son of Jonah)
46. Two ships	Ditto	Luke, VI, 4
47. Chose Simon, James, and John, fishers	Ditto	Luke, VI, 4
48. Miraculous draft of fishes	No mention of fishes or fishers	Luke, V, 6, John, XXI, 6
49. Fishers (Apostles)	No mention of fish or fishers	Matt., IV, 18, Mark, I, 10, Luke, V, John, XXI, 7
50. Feeds 5,000 men besides women and children on 5 loaves and 2 fishes	No mention of this	Matt., XIV, 15, XV, 32
51. Tribute from fishes' mouth	No mention of fish	Matt., XVII, 27
52. Fed 4,000 on 7 loaves and a few small fishes	Small cakes but no fishes, *Aryan Sun Myths*	Matt., XV, 34

Incidents.	Christna.	Christos.
53. Bruising head of serpent	*Asiatic Researches,* I, Higgins' *Anacalypta,* II, Bunsen's *Angel Messiah,* p. 39	Corinthians, Revelations, etc.
54. Transfigured before Disciples	Williams' *Hinduism,* p. 215	Matt., XVII, Mark, IX, 2, Luke, IX, 29, John, I, 14, 2 Peter, I, 16, John, XIII
55. Meekest of beings	Monier Williams' *Hind.,* p. 144	John, XIII
56. Alpha and Omega	*Geeta Lect.,* X, p. 86	Rev., I, 8-11, XXII, 13, XXI, 6
57. Crucified with arms extended, marks on hands, feet and side	Moors' *Hindu Pantheon* Inman's *Ancient Faith,* Vol. I, p. 411	Gospels
58. Sun darkened at crucifixion, consoled thief and hunter	*Progress of Religious Ideas,* I, 71	Matt., XXII

Incidents.	Christna.	Christos.
59. Pierced	Arrow, *Vishnu Purana,* p. 162	Spear, etc., Gospels
60. Descended into Hell 61. Rose from the dead	Bonwick's *Egyptian Belief,* 168 *Indian Antiquities,* II, 85 Dupui's *Origin of Religious Beliefs,* 240, Higgins' *Ana,* II, 142–145	Christian Creed Matt., XXVIII, Creed, etc., Mark, XVI, Luke, XXIV, John, XX
62. Ascended into Heaven	Bonwick's *Egypt. Beliefs,* 168 *Asiatic Researches,* I, 259, 261	Acts, I, 9
63. Many saw him ascend 64. Will come again, warrior on white horse, sun and moon will be darkened, stars fall from the firmament	*Hist. Hind.,* II, 466–473 *Hist. Hind.,* II, 497–503 Williams' *Hinduism,* 108 *Prog. Relig. Ideas,* I, 75	Gospels Revelations, VI, 2

Incidents.	Christna.	Christos.
65. Judge on last day		Matt., XXIV, 31
66. Had a beloved Disciple. Arjuna was both the cousin and beloved Apostle of Christna; but Jesus had two Johns — John the Baptist, his cousin, and John the beloved Apostle	*Oriental Religions*, p. 504 Arjuna Bhagavat These two names are really identical, " John " and " The John "	John John, XIII, 23
67. Creator of all things	*Gheeta*, p. 52	John, I, 3, 1 Corinthians, VIII, 6, Ephesians, III, 9
68. Transfigured, shining		Matt., XVII, 1–6
69. Second person in Trinity	Williams' *Hinduism*, (1) Ancient of days, Brama (2) Eternal one, far off (3) God on earth, Christna	Ancient of days, Father eternal, far off Son Christ—God on earth Holy Ghost, Ruach

Incidents.	Christna.	Christos.
	(4) Vishnu, fertile principle, female symbol, dove	Fertile principle, female symbol, dove
70. After resurrection eats fried or broiled fish	No fish reference. "Do this in remembrance of me"	Luke, XXIV, 42, 42 John, XXI, 13
71. After resurrection causes miraculous draft of fishes	No fish reference	John XXI, 6,
72. Light of the worlds	Williams' Hinduism, p. 213	John, VIII, 12
73. Predicts his own death	Hist. Hind., II, 275	Gospels
74. Walking over a river or sea	Hist. Hind., II, 331	Matt., XIV, 25–27

There are many minor identical sayings, incidents, and statements, which clearly prove that the Christos was a close Roman copy of the Christna of the Hindoos.

N

There was a further complication which created a great difficulty in formulating a clearly-defined system of religion, and that was the recognition by the more enlightened nations of the northern hemisphere, that the sun was the upholder of life on earth, beneficent god, man's true saviour from death or the evil of winter, and the various feasts, sacraments, and holy days of the churches were controlled by the sun's relation to the earth. It was clearly seen, especially by northern nations, that without the sun's fructifying influence death would ensue, so the sun was always the " saviour," and the chief god in the heavenly hierarchy, who, born a weak babe at the New Year, crossed over annually at the Spring equinox, to the salvation of mankind in northern nations. The writer of the Old Testament drew a clear picture of the sun as the god of the Hebrews in Exodus, XXIV, 10–17, which I have quoted, but which I repeat, it is so important, where they " saw the God of Israel, and there was under his feet as it were a paved work of sapphire stone, and as it were the body of heaven in its clearness," and at verse 17, " The sight of the glory of the Lord was like a devouring fire on the top of the mount in the eyes of the Children of Israel." No better description of the sun in a blue sky could

be found. So the Romans here describe the
Children of Israel as sun-worshippers. This
complication can be found in the religions of all
lands—the sun was the upholder of life and the
beneficent power which ripened fruits and grain
for food, and so sustained life and marked the
seasons, in fact, a friendly god—man's benefactor
—he was also the upholder of life and even the
creator, but these early thinkers could not imagine
the sun as the begetter of life, hence they had a
double-sided religion, with the sun as the sky god,
but sex-creation, represented by a name founded
on the creation of new life as seen on earth, and
represented by the combined male and female
organs, or a hermaphroditic god, embodying their
idea of the "creative" side of the great god on
earth. This god, a god of fertility or of procreation,
was generally prayed to under a model of the male
organ, as in the case of Jacob's pillow, pillar, or
stone, which we call "phallic" worship from the
Latin for the male organ, the phallus (from the
Hindoo pala, as I have already explained). Sex
creation, however, as on earth, was represented
by the male and female organs combined, as in
the Lingam-Yoni altar of India, of which I
illustrate several forms, or by hermaphroditic
beings having the two sex organs in one person,

FIG. 45A.—Lingam-Yoni Altar, with gods.

FIGS. 46 AND 47.—Lingam Yoni Altars.

as in the Indian Ardha-Nari Eswara, the right side male, left side female, or Omphale (womb or woman, and phallus), or any of the double-sexed gods of religious myth. " Hermaphroditic " simply describes the union of Hermes (Mercury, the lively god) and Aphrodite or Venus, the seductive goddess in the act of producing life.

As intelligence increased, the more enlightened nations felt that the very fact that the sun's return could be calculated for the recurrence of the seasons showed that " he " was not a " free-willed " god, but was " ruled " by some greater but hidden power—the " Unknown God." When the Chinese and the Babylonian astronomers, and later the Egyptians, got up tables of the sun's movements, showing his mechanical character, he was destroyed to the educated as a living god. In fact, astronomy destroyed the sun-god idea, as Persia's poet-astronomer (Omar Khayyám) sings :—

" And that inverted bowl we call the sky,
　Where under crawling cooped we live and
　　die,
　Lift not your hands to it for help, for it
　As impotently moves as you or I."　(LXXII).

The Protestant Church will require to drop its present interpretation of the Bible as the word of an all-wise god, or it will suffer shipwreck when the true origin of the Holy Scriptures is known, and that will not be long delayed, as the facts I am detailing in this book are becoming wide-spread through my earlier volumes. That is the reason that the Bible is forbidden to Catholics, although it is claimed as the medium on which is founded the Roman Catholic religion. The opposite is the truth. The Romans composed their Bible and then tried to control mankind by making it " catholic " or universal.

But no church lives entirely on theories, or even on beliefs, and only the few serious thinkers reason on religious subjects. The whole attitude of the Roman Church is to debase its votaries as independent thinkers. The kneeling position while the priest prays is one of degradation, and the confessional undermines all the mental strength of the individual by depending on another instead of being master of his own fate.

The Church lives mainly on ritual, and on the belief that *the* deadly sin is doubt, if that doubt pertains to any of the priest's statements. It inculcates that this, that, or the other thing, is " holy," and that prayers for the dead will help the dead man's " soul " in " another world," with swinging of censors, chaunting of Psalms, and making secret or " holy " signs, and so on—these are the real props of the " foundations of belief," and the priest's power is most complete in those religions whose ritual plays the greatest part. It is a great crime to ask questions about " holy " things—a crime at one time punished with death, as these questions only embarrass the priest. The Protestant Church lacks all these props, and it will either become a " non-supernatural-belief " body, teaching only a religion of kindness, which is the only creed worth following, or it will become extinct. Protestants are the cream of the peoples, and they read, so their acquaintance with the results of scientific investigation will undermine their faith in the " big man " god, and an " after-life," and they will turn their whole energies to bettering *this* life.

All " revealed " faiths are bound to die, as the falsity of the priests' statements is always exposed by the more advanced thinkers, owing to their receptivity of new ideas and the results of scientific research.

For instance, the learned and reverend authors of the *Encyc. Bib.* have treated the Jesus miracles of walking on the waters, feeding thousands, etc., as " childish " fables, and have declared that Peter and Paul were merely " pen " names, or lay figures on which the true authors of the New Testament, the Roman ecclesiastics, hung their religious disquisitions—in fact, that the whole narrative is fiction. That was always my opinion. The artificial sources of the names Peter and Paul are very apparent.

Petros or Peter is the Greek for Tsur, the " rock that begat thee," the phallus of the circumcision-loving nations, or tribes of the Old Testament, and Paul, the pala, pul, or pal, the phallus, a name derived from India, where the male reproductive organ is called the pala, pawl, etc. The purpose of the introduction of these two lay figures was to conduct a discussion as to the necessity of carrying out Jehovah's " covenant," by cutting off the foreskin of the phallus, as practised by one section of the Church and opposed by the other. Circumcision was abandoned.

As to the famous Pauline Epistles, the *Encyc. Bib.* tells us, as I have already noted, that " there are none of them by Paul " (col. 3,625).

These Oxford divines give us to understand that Peter and Paul are literary creations of mere pen names or "lay figures," on which to gather speeches or points of dogmatic religion. Not one of the

fourteen famous Epistles bearing the Pauline name
is by Paul (*Encyc. Bib.*, col. 3,625). In fact, the
Encyc. Bib., the great work of Oxford scholarship,
is very clear, emphatic, and final in its statements,
all founded on long and very recondite research by
the greatest of all nations' scholars. They have
totally destroyed the Bible as a Holy Book of
God. I am extremely desirous to make this study
a short, clear résumé of the work of clearing away
the poisonous edicts of " official " religion, that
I only quote decisive statements here and there,
otherwise this work would be too long and too
expensive for ordinary readers. The enormous
loss incurred in the production of the *Encyc. Bib.*
shows that readers want decisive statements
without long discussion. But the *Encyc. Bib.*
has cleared away the mass of vague Jesuitical
statement—I shall not say reasoning—a work of
extreme utility which has the grateful thanks of
all scholars.

One last quotation to clear the ground.

In col. 3,625, the *Encyc. Bib.*, after a long and
very searching inquiry into the Pauline literature,
states : " Neither the fourteen nor thirteen, nor
nine or ten, nor yet even the four, so long universally regarded as unassailable. They are all
without distinction pseudepigrapha " [sham writ-

ings]. This word accurately describes not only the Epistles but the whole Bible. I must refer my readers to my "Sex Symbolism," Vol. I, Ch. V, pp. 259–298, for a brief résumé of the splendidly scholarly destruction of the whole Pauline story and literature, as I have gathered there much of the *Encyc. Bib.'s* statements, but I recommend students to go to that great work itself to enable them to appreciate the sweeping and meticulous destruction of the work of the real founders of Christianity—the writers, priests, scribes or scholars who wrote the famous Epistles, which are masterpieces of poisonous Jesuitical sophistry.

As I have sketched in my opening chapters, the collection of sacred books from savage tribes by Ptolemy Soter at Alexandria, afterwards removed to Galilee, to aid in the composition of a " bible " for a universal or " catholic " religion under the Romans, we will now look into the use made of these old manuscripts in framing the symbolism of the Bible names and narrative, which were only produced in its authoritative state over five hundred years later.

The grave, bearded figure of Serapis, of Egypt, was used as the early portrait of Jesus, as were also the statues of Isis with her babe as the Virgin Mary. The actual Isis statues were at first freely used throughout Italy and Greece, right through to Asia Minor, but gradually the new sculptors produced the Virgin Mary with her babe as we know her.

The service of the Church was naturally given the highest place by the clergy, so we find that Mary Magdalene had chosen the " better part " as a temple harlot to serve the priests' lusts and to bring in revenue, as compared with Martha, who was the good, homely housewife, troubled about " many things " necessary to make a comfortable home, whereas Mary had chosen a " better part," namely, caressing the Church's " feet," and we know the universal use of the word " foot " in a phallic sense, " hair " being also a " secret " sign, and Luke very carefully emphasises that " one thing was needful," namely, a revenue for the churches or temples, and we know that the entire temple revenues were dependent on the prostitution of the " sacred " women engaged in harlotry, ending in a cruel and early death from syphilis, or, as " John " puts it, anointing the " feet " of the Lord with ointment and wiping his " feet " with her " hair " (complete subjection to the degrading " offices " of the temple harlots). Now she, Mary of Magdala, Mary of the " Almond," symbolic term for the *membrum femininum*, who had " much loved," a euphuism for service as a temple prostitute, was one of those women whose hire constituted the " whole religion " of the Children of Israel (see Judges, V, 6 and 7, and the *Encyc. Bib.*, cols. 1,511 and 1,512, also 1,965, 1,966, and many other enlightening passages; see also my " Sex Symbolism," Vol. I, pp. 285-6-7 and 388-394, and also the *Encyc. Bib.*, cols. 338 and 756).

The name Mary in Hebrew (Mari) belongs to a root meaning to excite, and " Mari " is " she who excites the god to action "—a theory held of all " gods "—as without the female they could not create. As the hire of the temple prostitutes constituted the " entire revenue " of these temples (*Encyc. Bib.*), Jesus is made to praise Mary as having chosen the " better part," providing the temples with funds by caressing the " feet " of the devotees.

The *Encyc. Bib.* says, of the orgiastic feasts which were accompanied by total nudity of body and promiscuous sexual intercourse (as still practised in India), " *the entire religious observances of the nation were contained in these feasts* " (*Encyc. Bib.*, col. 1,512). [For a complete proof of the phallic meaning of " feet," see Forlong's " Rivers of Life "; but for a true illustrated account of the universal rule of the most crass phallic ideas in Rome one must have access to Payne Knight's " Worship of Priapus " (now very rare, but available in the special room of the British Museum Library)].

To return to early religions of a higher type, we find Siddartha, a young Hindoo Prince, tired of the futilities of the Court, after begetting a son, as he was bound in honour and by his religion to do, went out into the world to wander in lonely places seeking "nearness to God." This was about 400 B.C.

He taught a religion of kindness in most beautiful phrases, and lived an austere life, leaving a fine record of his gentle teaching to his followers in such phrases as " Let a man leave anger, let him forsake pride, let him overcome all bondage. Let a man overcome anger by love, let him overcome evil by good, let him overcome the greedy by liberality, the liar by truth. He abused me, he beat me, he defeated me, he robbed me ; in those who harbour such thoughts hatred will never cease. For hatred does not cease by hatred at any time ; hatred ceases by love." This beautiful teaching, the result of wandering among the poor, took root in the gentle Hindoo, and has remained the core of their religion to the present day.

Asoka, a monarch of India, proposed to make Siddartha's gentle teaching the basis for universal religion of kindness, and he sent out missionaries to convert the world.

But, as we all know, such is the hardness and unkindness of mankind, owing to the pressure of population, and the consequent struggle for mere existence among the masses, that a religion of kindness at that date was like sowing good seed in a barren soil.

Besides that, the local priesthood virulently opposed any change, and the whole revenues of the temples were derived from the hire of the sacred prostitutes—by the utter degradation and often of death from frightful incurable diseases of the poor Magdalenes, or " white slaves."   Rome saw the decay of the old gods, Jupiter, Juno, etc., and, having conquered Europe and Asia up to India—conquests she could not hold by force alone, she saw that a new religion was an essential to government.   But it must be a State religion, with all the revenues and power over the individual vested in the State, and not frittered away by the rivalry of many famous but competing " shrines."

So Rome decided to combine the two great levers—a religion, nominally of kindness, based on Siddartha's teaching, but retaining the old symbolic phallic god names of all countries, backed up by threats of punishment here and hereafter—inflicted by hell-fire after death, but also by immediate punishment inflicted by Roman arms directed by the Bishops, Archbishops, Cardinals,

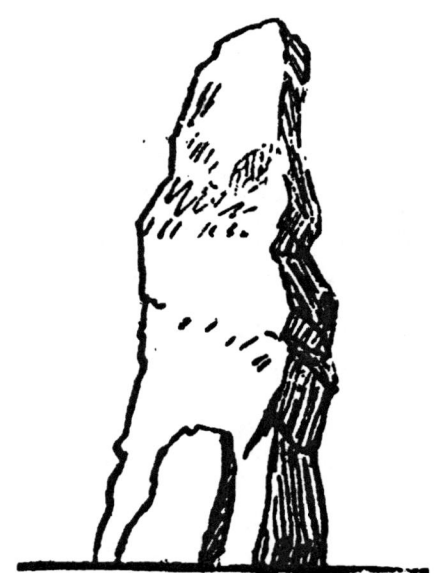

FIG. 48.—Phallic Rock.

etc., directly from Rome. They also invented the infernal engines of confession and ex-communication, by which men who refused to obey—often betrayed by confessions extracted from their women-folk—were driven out by ex-communication to die a miserable death or made to recant by

long-drawn-out torture by infernal machines, or the most terrible of all deaths, burning at the stake for all "unbelievers." These infernal measures generally maintained the power of Rome, but when they failed there were always sufficient soldiers to over-awe the small communities which rebelled, or which desired to return to the "ancient gods."

They even slaughtered the recalcitrant priests in thousands, and Tacitus relates a great slaughter of British Druidical priests on the Island of Anglesea, where the Roman soldiers had "rounded them up," and slaughtered them, the men along with their women, who probably acted as oracles encouraging rebellion. By having a supreme Father, Papa or Pope at Rome, who controlled all the priesthood, any recalcitrant king, governor, or official who attempted to defy Rome's power, could be removed by an edict of the Pope and dethroned by the same power which had enthroned him.

Thus was the terrible and powerful engine of the Inquisition imposed on the Roman Empire by the clerics.

On the other hand, the Indian Prince Siddartha's humane and gentle teaching had gained many believers in kindness instead of fear, through the

o

efforts of the Indian monarch Asoka, who had
tried to spread the religion of kindness and
humanity, and the learned men of Alexandria,
under Ptolemy Soter, knew of the efforts made
to promulgate the gentle teaching of goodness
and kindness practised by the Indian Prince. A
great college of pundits was being established at
Tyberya, in the lake of that name in northern
Palestine, to study the great question of a universal
religion for the whole Roman Empire. As any
religion—to be universal—must not interfere with
the feasts and joyous celebrations connected with
the seasons of the year, the return of the sun, the
Spring, the harvest, etc., the Romans decided to
base their new religion on these recurring celebrations, and so they called their college and
town, established for the creation of the new or
combined religion, by the suitable name " Galilee,"
meaning " the circle of the year." They named both
town and lake by the new title, but so strong is
custom that the Arabs still call the town and
lake " Tyberya." The new religion, evolved by
many centuries of work at " Galilee," was one
founded on symbolical names building up a story
of the progress of the world, symbolised in one
supposed little clan called " Hebrews," in a land
to which they gave a new name, and as this religion

was one in which the two sexes, or sex organs, symbolised gods, eternal life, and all sacred things, they called the land " Palestine," the " stan " or " land " of the pala, the Hindoo name for the male organ. Here we have the key to the Bible mythology which dealt with the two sources or upholders of " life," first the sun, so well described in Ex., XXIV, 10, as the " God of Israel," and second the two sex organs, out of the names of which we shall find nearly all other names produced and out of which were produced all the paraphernalia of worship.

The new religion was called the universal religion of the Romans, or in their cryptic rendering the " Roman Catholic Religion," " catholic " being, as I have already told, derived from two Greek words, Kata and Holos, Kata meaning " throughout " or " entire," and Holos " whole," meaning throughout the whole world, or a " universal religion."

As it was partly composed in a specially invented speech or language which the Romans called " Hebrew," and the other part in Greek, both " difficult " languages, and none of it in Latin, it shows clearly that it was designedly written in these languages so that neither the Romans nor any other nation could read both books—not even scribes or priests, but only the Roman-trained Church scholars ; so the people could only know of their contents through the Roman priests; in fact, the Church of Rome has always forbidden laymen from reading or attempting to read the Bible.

But the Roman Bible pertained only to one land, and it ought to have been called the Palestinian Bible, both Old and New Testaments having been staged there, or it might have been called the " Hebrew and Greek " or Græco-Hebraic religion, as there is essentially no Latin in the books.

Still it was the Roman Catholic religion, because the whole composition was undertaken to aid Rome in governing foreign nations, and the scheme was that of Rome to gain universal dominion over all lands on which this new religion was imposed.

The grave, bearded figure of the Egyptian god Serapis (Hebrew Seraph, or Seraphim, serpent columns) was used as the early portrait of the son of God called IesU (our Jesus, but pronounced Yaisu) or the " God made flesh for us," as is re-iterated twelve times (the sun's journey over the twelve signs of the Zodiac) in the Epistles of the New or Greek Testament, and mentioned as the " Word made flesh " in John, I, 14. It was supposed to be an inspired message from a god to the Hebrews, but it was not called the " Hebrew "

universal religion, but the "Roman," clearly showing that it was a product of Roman governmental industry.

A series of great Œcumenical Councils was held —"Œcumenical" being a pompous Greek term meaning the "whole habitable world," in fact, it is simply another way of saying "total," "complete" or "universal," like "Catholic," so here again we have Rome's claim to universal dominion, and to impose their fraudulent composition of a religion, made out of "sex" or "phallic" words, on the whole world.

There is not one word telling us how these scriptures were obtained, or proving their honest origin, and nothing was allowed to leak out as to the method of compiling this curious collection of "doubtful" tales out of crude religious or phallic stories of adultery, onanism, incest, polygamy and dishonest cunning; but as the priests were purely brothel keepers (see Leckie and all ancient records) and gained all their wealth from "letting out" their Nuns (fish women) or temple harlots for hire to all and sundry, we can scarcely be surprised at the contents of their Bible. As I have already pointed out, the close female companion of the supposed Son of God, IesU, or Jesus, as we erroneously call him, was a temple prostitute or

" almond " woman (almond being an ancient and universal symbol for the *membrum femininum*). She is described in Luke, VIII, 12, " and the twelve were with him, and certain women which had been healed of evil spirits and infirmities " [sexual disease], " Mary Magdalene, out of whom went seven devils."

Her name, Mari Magdalene, is full of significance. Again two languages are used. In Hebrew Mari means " She who urges the god to action " (a phrase applied to the wives of all creators), and applicable to Mary [Mari], the mother of Jesus. Magdalene means " almond " woman, referring to her sex organ being always at the service of the priests. The almond is a very old symbol for the *membrum femininum*, its shape being more appropriate than the " ring " of Yima.

" Rod and almond " (Jeremiah, I, 11) mean the male and female *pudenda* or " shameful things." So Mary was, as all serious Bible students now admit, a temple prostitute, and her title of Mary " of the almond " and her " seven devils " refer to her profession as a " temple " or " dedicated " woman or " nun," and the awful diseases to which the promiscuous prostitution of the temples gave rise. We read of emerods in their " secret parts " in Deut., XXVIII, 27, and in 1 Sam., V, 6, and in

FIG 51. MARY MAGDALENE

verse 19, fifty thousand and three score and ten were smitten with emerods, syphilis, owing to meddling with the Ark, the supreme symbol of " woman," verily, as the writer remarks, " a great slaughter," so they were not only " smitten " but they died (see also the Midianite women). " Rod and almond " are identical with " Zakar " or " Zikar and Nekebah," sword, dagger, or " piercer " and " womb " of Genesis, for " male and female " in Gen., I, 27. I have already quoted Jeremiah as announcing his mission as a priest as " seeing rod and almond."

So IesU is associated through all his ministry with the temple prostitute, as were all priests. Without the hire of the prostitutes the priests could not exist, and they would have had to " turn to " and do some work for an honest living. No cure for syphilis was then known, so the prostitutes' life must have been a hell ending in a painful death. (See Deut., IV, 3, Numb., XXXI, 16, and my " Christianity," pp. 230 et seq., or my " Sex Symbolism "). These prostitutes were called Nuns, meaning " fish " women, the sun being in the constellation of Pisces, the Fishes, at the time of the Christos and Christna, called IesU, and his life is full of fishermen and fish miracles. They are still called " Nuns " by the " Romans " in

Britain, but whether they are used by the priests or are simply " almoners " is quite unknown to anyone outside the priest ring.   But that they are kept quite isolated is very suspicious. I think that the seclusion of any sane, healthy people should be against the law of all civilised countries.   They don't attempt to seclude men by women's power. We have no record of how all the various " books " of the Bible were composed, or from what quarter came the instructions as to the lines on which the fictitious " Hebrew " history was to be built, but no doubt there were numerous contributors during the 400 or more years they were at the work, and an enormous amount of trial literature would have been rejected before the authorities found something which has been defined as " needful and apt."   But a long study of the various books of the Bible has caused me to cease to wonder that it took so long a time to create a new alphabet and language of quite unnatural origin, and therefore even now " vague and difficult."   We have no information how the books were composed, but we have a series of so-called Œcumenical Councils pretending to debate all sorts of recondite points of the philosophy of religion and elaborate discussions about Church organisation, the standing and

discipline of the officials, and I have no doubt
learned disputes down to hair-splitting disquisitions as to how many angels could stand on a
needle's point, but no word—not even a whisper
—of the manufacture of a new language in a new
alphabet, creating this great system of sex symbolism and phallic nomenclature, which was a fitting
frame for the organised business of brothel keeping
which was the Church's practice and chief source of
revenue for sixteen hundred years, and before
Christianity for thousands of years, religion was
coition (see Lucian's " Syrian Goddess "). We
gather from many sources (some very dubious)
that the Old and New Testaments began to be
constructed about the end of the second century
of our era, and in the fourth century Eusebius
was busy with his final " Canon," which was
said to be fixed about 382, but it took over 300
years' further time to " fine down " and correct
the new alphabet and symbolism used for
thousands of symbolised names in the Bible, and
to bring down the phallic nomenclature of the
Romans, so widely employed in the construction
of the Hebrew Old Testament so as to be still
applicable to the New Testament (now in Greek),
which the Romans constructed as the mainspring
of the great and wonderful machine they were

designing and constructing. They utilised the fables and "holy literatures" of the extreme Eastern nations, China and India, as well as the many modifications of words and names which had crept in during the Western migration of the Asiatic god-names. We must not forget that the particle Di, as in Divine, or De, also Ti, Te, The, as in Theology or in Deity, and the Roman Deus, came from China, while "fleshly" god-names come from the Indian pala, the male organ, as in pale (a Stob), pole, pillar, also palace, Palestine, etc. We write names quite erroneously in the corrupt West, writing Jesus, "Jesus," for Iesu, which original, however, we still reverently inscribe on our tombstones (Iesu Hominum Salvator, I.H.S.).

We must not forget that the Romans wrote our Bible—not the Hebrews (they are a myth) nor the Greeks—so the "Church" or Roman spelling is the correct form. It may be that the reason for using J for I all through the English Bible was the ignorance of the English "divines." They saw the German I in, say, our Joseph (which should be Ioseph, or better as to pronunciation Yoseph), printed with the German I, which has a crook like our J, and they may have slavishly copied this, or they may have suspected the true meaning of the I, and been glad to disguise it by copying the

German letter.   But in any case the substitution of J for I is a capital disguise in "dangerous" names.   IO is clearly Yima's piercer, or pillar, and ring—two sexes to produce all life, but JO is quite innocent of any such meaning.   I sometimes think that the great difficulty all scholars find in making a sensible translation of Hebrew, owing to its being a purely manufactured language and not one of natural growth, was felt by the ignorant English "divines," and they simply rendered Luther's Bible into English without any reference to Hebrew.   That would account for the constant error of J for the Hebrew I.   So close is the English to the German translation that it is very like a slavish copy.

"J" was admirably suited to disguise the alphabetical symbolism employed by the Romans to create their god-names.   This is a moot point, but in any case it succeeded in its disguising rôle very well.   For instance, the very simple name (simple when considered symbolically) Jehovah has very little similarity with true name of the Hebrew god created by the Romans, IHOH, which they called the sacred Tetragrammaton, the "divine four letters," or four-letter sign. I mention this "ineffable" name as I have fully dealt with the secret meaning of the three letters

involved in this " name "—as well as the letters
U and V, which were identical under the Romans
and expressed by one sign in the artificial Hebrew,
the letter Vav (or Waw), as some writers express it.
We have seen the reason for eliminating the letters
O, U and V, as these were the letters sumbolically
representing the female or her sex organ, and they
also eliminated the pala or pillar letter I, symbol
of the male organ and represented it as a comma (,)
so as to make all these double-sexed names mean-
ingless to the eye.   (See IHOH in Index.)

But it is irreverent and dangerous to change
holy words or signs, so IHS (Iesu Hominum Salvator) is still used, even by Protestants, for Jesus
Saviour of Men (or Jesus of men the Saviour),
so Iesu is the true name of the Protestant Saviour,
not " Jesus," as has been abundantly proved by
our present study. The use of the letters I and
O (or U and V) to represent double-sex (or the
creative organs) was universal, as expressed by
the Persians, who said that Yima (the earth Lord)
was given a dagger or a piercer and a ring, with
which to create all life. The use of IO in all
countries, as male and female, caused the Romans
to suppress them in the new Bible and, as U and
V were used in place of O, they made OU and V
into a staff, with a dot differently placed for each,

and they made I (the rod or pillar, pala) into a comma and so destroyed all phallic significances.

Our Bible was a growth of centuries under the Romans, designed to fill a long-desired rôle of an authoritative " word of God," and all sorts of versions were produced and criticised by the Bishops at Constantinople between the second century A.D. till 692 A.D., when a final conference was held at Constantinople, or, as it should be spelt, Constantinopal, as " opal " is a double-sexed word applied to holy towns in the East. This city had become more representative of the Roman power than Rome itself. Here, " in trullo," under the dome—of the palace, not of St. Sophia (which, as representing " wisdom," would have been very appropriate), but, as its dome had collapsed, and although rebuilt and superbly decorated, as may still be seen, it was no longer used for Conferences—here was held the last great Conference, the "quin-sext" (fifth and sixth combined) at which the final form of the Bible was approved for issue.   It is most important to note that during all the centuries during which the work of creating a new " word of God" on disguised phallic symbolism was on hand, when most important decisions must have been taken as to the basis on which the creation of all the symbolic names were to be founded, there is not a whisper as to the elaborate system of symbolism which I have gradually unravelled and which I uncover or prove in detail in this my final volume, the result of fifty years of constant study of the Christian scriptures and all their expositories and apologetics.

The clerics at Constantinople threw dust in the people's eyes by pseudo-learned reports on discussions on doctrine, on the positions, names, and duties of Church officials, on the dress and paraphernalia of worship, and no doubt "split hairs" on such questions as to how many angels could stand on a needle's point, but, I repeat, not one word, not even a whisper, as to the construction of their double-sexed names for gods, angels, prophets, kings, priests, patriarchs, and even common men and women, in their symbolic tale. They seemed to think that because they were composing a holy book with double-sexed or "creative" gods they must give equally "holy" names to all the "characters" they introduced. One sensible matter was agreed upon in relation to the position of the heavenly bodies. The whole round of the Zodiac must be considered with its 12 signs roughly corresponding to the 12 months of the year, and when the sun entered into a new

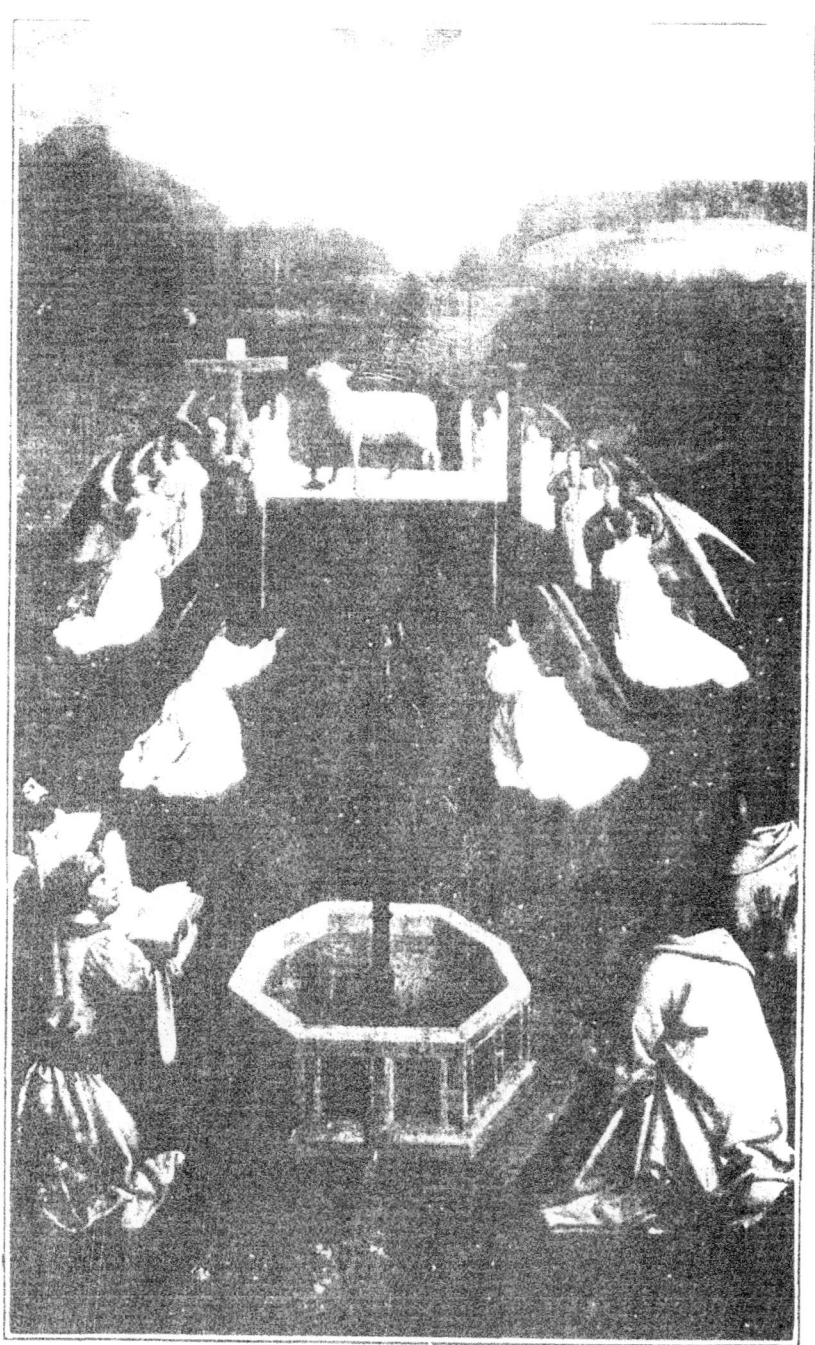

sign by the slow change called the " precession of the equinoxes," which slowly displaced the equinoctial position by the space of one sign in the 12 of the Zodiac in about 2,150 years (or 2,200 years, as the limits of the " sign " constellations were very vague), there must have been great disturbance of mind when the precession finally displaced the old sign and the State astronomers or priests announced a new name for the " god " or " sacred name."   Or it may be that some nations, probably the Egyptians, held great re-joicings in order to placate the new god, just arriving, who might be represented like Jesus as the son of the old god, bearing, of course, a new name.   *The Romans separated their religion from all Zodiacal fables.*   The disappearance of the old sign of, say, the Twins, represented by twin pillars everywhere (the Roman Gemini) with its Castor and Pollux, was accompanied by the adoption of a new name, the Bull (Taurus), so grandly portrayed by the Assyrians, as seen in the British Museum, or in the double-sexed Bull of the Minoans, which was called the Minotaur, " Min," the ithyphallic (shameful) god of Egypt, with the female symbol " O " coupled with the Bull, " Taur(us) "=Minotaur, a name which has puzzled many explorers, and was not dealt with

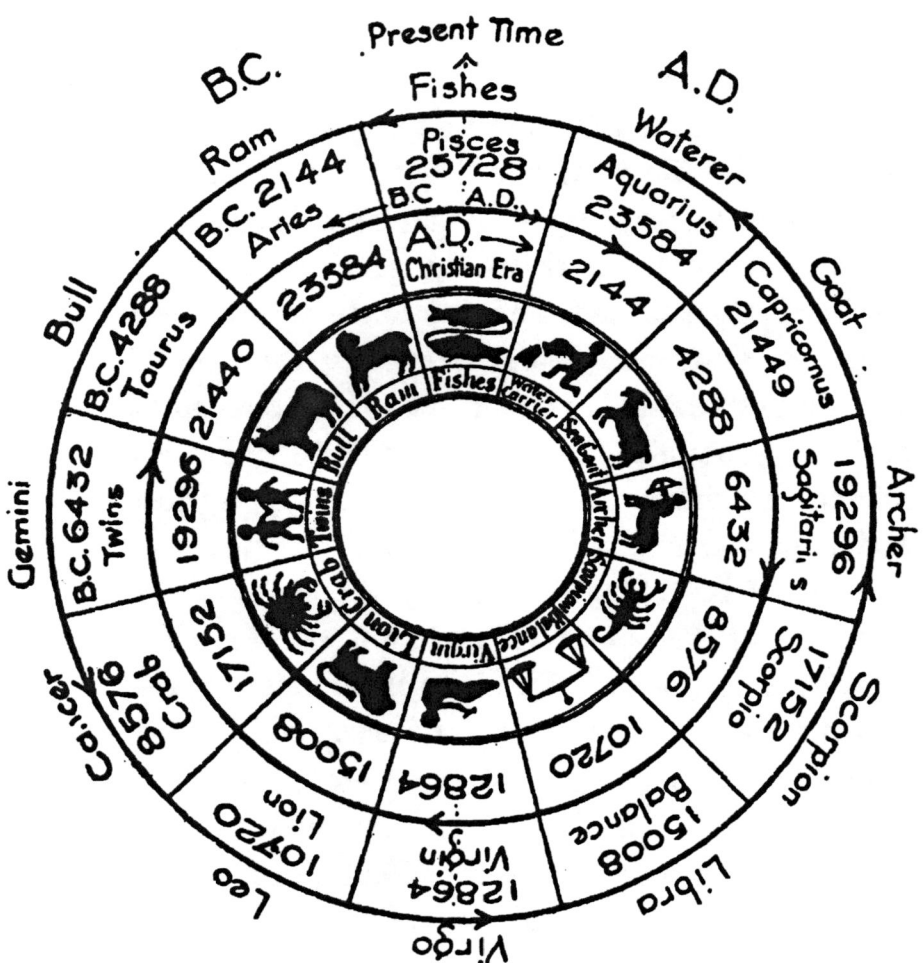

FIG. 53.—PROCESSION OF THE EQUINOXES.

Times of Signs of Zodiac before and after Christian Era.
Dates.   Inner Circle increasing numbers of A.D. years.
          Outer Circle   „   „   of B.C. years.
All from the present time.

FIG 54 MINOAN SERPENT PRIESTESS

by Sir Arthur Evans as fully as it should be. The Minoans have the same name, their land must have had a double-sexed god Min-o, and I lean to the opinion that they obtained this name from Egypt, as the Egyptian sculpture is shameless in its naked "rudeness" (Fig. 38, p. 116), showing an ancient invention ; while the Minoans, although having phallic names and exhibiting the serpent-symbol for the phallus, have their goddess fully clothed, only exposing her breasts to show her fertility. Perhaps they used the mammary organs, instead of phallus, testes, or yoni, as a life-giving symbol, but in any case the goddess also held the serpent as her holy sign, and the serpent is always the phallus, thus forming with the female a double-sexed or creative combination.

To avoid the disturbance on the change of name of the god on a change of constella-tion, the ecclesiastics agreed to cease using the signs of the astronomic Zodiac emblems as the personality of the god, and decided that the lamb or ram should be superseded by the figure of a man kneeling and adoring a cross. This symbolised two different things, the *first* being the sun's crossing of the equator at the Spring equinox, and saving man from a dead world, or perpetual winter in the northern hemisphere,

P

which was the " thinking " half of the world, and the second the phallus or life-giver, which Colenso and all scholars proved to be an " eternal-life " symbol like the fleur-de-lys, the broad arrow, the Prince of Wales' feathers, the pyx and most of the phallic columns, which were generally erected with two small stones, one at each side, so representing the phallus and testes. (pp. 72-76.)

This worship, or paying homage and rejoicing, to the sun or god at the equinoctial crossing signalised man's escape from the cold and death of winter, as without the heat of the " northing " sun, death would reign in the northern hemisphere.

The abandonment of the Zodiac signs for the phallic cross (sign of eternal life) was slow, and for a time the holy sign was Pisces, into which constellation the sun passed at the time when the Romans were creating their IesU, the Christ—hence his Apostle fishermen and miraculous feeding with two small fishes, the Zodiacal sign of that date, and the fish sign, " two fishes," was cut on tombstones till about 400 A.D. He also eats fish before his Ascension, and says "do this in remembrance of me." The fish sign seems to have lost its popularity about 400 A.D., or a little later. No other sign replaced it, simply pious inscriptions. So long do superstitious signs linger, that you will see the sign of the Ram with the equinoctial sign of the cross on its shoulder in the " Temple," between the Strand and the Victoria Embankment, to this day, a relic of over 2,000 years ago, so the cross was a religious symbol thousands of years before IesU Christos.

I have given some lists of names derived from one word, Tsur, as an example of the Romans' creation of names of gods and men, and the reader may continue the process indefinitely, as there are 7,000 artificial names in the Bible story, but to me the tracing of all their origins is not worth the trouble.

CONCLUSION

IF I were asked to describe the religion of the books forced on us by the Romans, " setting down nothing in malice," I would be bound to state that my studies and the *Encyc. Bib.* and Hebrew lexicons show me that :—All the gods and very nearly all the characters in the Bible are hermaphroditic, or have names composed of letters indicating double-sex, so that one individual can create life, having the necessary two sexes. The Old Testament is not a Hebrew book, it was not written by Jews, nor does it represent their history. It is a purely Roman creation, to aid the conquering Romans in governing the countries which they had invaded, and its narrative is pure fiction.

The supposed history of Palestine and the Hebrews' intromissions with their god, are pure " romance," written to aid the Romans in governing the peoples they had conquered, by building up an ancient sacred history. It is entirely imaginary from beginning to end, and utterly untrue, and its gods are mere symbols. Its gods, and names, are artificially composed of phallic groups of letters conveying a double-sex meaning to symbolise creative, holy, or god-like power. They consist of names only, and never had a real existence. Christianity is simply one of the many religious myths. The priests who composed it praise deceit, craftiness and cowardly theft, as in the story of Jacob and Esau. Further, I should say that the Old Testament is a purely pornographic or shameful production of a "high-place," or brothel-keeping clergy, and its ideas and symbolism are taken from Hindoo, Persian and Egyptian sources, which were all phallic, and written, as to the Old Testament, in a secret and invented script which never was, nor could be, spoken. This was invented by the Romans. Gods' names are groups of double-sexed letters indicating life-creative gods by the two sex organs. I would feel bound to state that the New or Greek Testament is not a true account of history, but again purely a product of Roman scholarship founded on Hindoo ideas and titles, merely using Greek to disguise its real meaning and origin. Its temples were brothels, like those all over the world at that time, and the Church's income was derived from the "white slave traffic." Jesus and all other characters are names composed of symbolic letters, and never had a real existence.

Both books have a purely cryptic character. Both are quite openly phallic, born in hot-beds of pornography, built on serpent and pillar worship, representing the male sex organ as the prime god-symbol, and the combined male and female sex organs as the "only living and true creative god."

The priests' income was derived from the degradation of women, who were held as brothel slaves, living a life of torture from the most painful of diseases, ending in a lingering, painful death, as told in the Old Testament.

The Roman Government Bible has not brought peace to the world, but truly "a sword" dripping with blood, and a world watered by rivers of women's tears. Happily, its reign is nearly over.

The *Encyc. Bib.* is indeed a great work. These Oxford scholars "builded better than they knew." By their bold researches they have blown away the miasmatic vapours of Jesuitical conspiracies, and let the fresh breezes of truth into the mental world of men.

Some of these men think they have raised an ugly giant to devour faith, but, as Ruskin very beautifully said of the danger of faith without reason, "It invests every evil passion of our nature with the aspect of an angel of light."

It is astonishing to what depths of immoral

symbolism the brothel-keeping Roman clergy sank in their Bible composing. Let anyone study the names in the lists of men and tribes so often catalogued in the Bible, such as those in Genesis, X, 13–14, or in 1st Chronicles, I, 11–12, and he will see to what depths of leering pornography the Roman clergy could descend.

The Bible is full of passages too gross for translation, and containing sex words connected with the Roman religion. This is not surprising, as their whole occupation and the income on which they subsisted seems devoted to and derived from the training and " letting out " of women for prostitution ; and this is the sacred record of the god whom the clergy ask us to fear and to adore.

The greater number of the 7,000 names in the Bible are derived from pornographic ideas, especially from the conjunction of the two sexes in every ingenious combination possible, as in the cases of Jehovah and Jesus. I give a few here in an Appendix.

We must remember that, their god-names being founded on the symbolic representation of the sex members in coition, it was natural that they took a similar course in creating names for men and women in their great " romance " of the

Hebrew race. No wonder that it took centuries to create a whole nation and its appropriate literature.

Faith was no kindly nurse of man's intellect but a barrier to progress, a true nightmare of horrors with its hell and fore-ordination and its absolutely cold-blooded ferocious god, well represented by the black-hooded " familiars " of that real hell, the "Inquisition." The Bible god, if he is omniscient, must know where every individual soul is going after the bodily death, and, therefore, knowingly and criminally creates men to have the pleasure of seeing them suffer in eternal hell fire— an awful fiend instead of a god, a fear-god to enslave men by a lying system, created by the priests to acquire universal dominion for Rome. All that terrible dream of miasmatic horrors of the Jesuitical Roman priesthood, the most poisonous fungus the world has ever known, will be swept away by modern science, and no doubt helped by the tree Oxford has planted.

It's a fine thing to think that our two universities have given us the two great desiderata of " freedom " and knowledge. Oxford thought that her researches would prove a solid foundation for the truth of the Holy Scriptures, but, like all useful serious research, these labours have uncovered hitherto unimagined facts which have broken up their "little systems which have their day and cease to be."

I notice a speech by Dr. Barnes, the Bishop of Birmingham, on October 13th, 1924, in which he prettily tells us he believes "God works through Newton and Darwin no less than through Isaiah and St. Paul" (neither of whom ever existed), which is at least a slight sign of "grace" from a prelate of the Church. The *Encyc. Bib.* says, with respect to the Canonical Pauline Epistles, the later criticism has learned to recognise that "*there are none of them by Paul*" (*Encyc. Bib.*, col. 3,625). But the *Encyc. Bib.* uses the word "mythical" in treating of the story of Moses, and the same great Oxford work says that Paul did not write any of the Epistles attached to his name, so he also is a myth, as there is now no evidence of his existence. But what does Dr. Barnes mean by "God?" Is it IHOH, male and female organs with testicles or ovaries, or "El Shaddai," the "micturating god," or Al or El, the phallic pillar god, or Tsur the "Rock that begat thee," or the Eli on whom IesU cried on the Cross? What and who is his God? Is he a man with a form and a brain like ourselves, or is he a "gas" or a "spirit"? If he thinks, must he not have a brain? Let us have a clear view of this " God " from those who assert his existence. *We see no guiding hand anywhere.* There is no interference from unknown sources. Elements and their compounds have no " free will "; in similar circumstances they inevitably yield the same results. Therefore I say to the clergy, what is your God? We see no interference and we see no intelligent governance. What then is your God, and what does he do? We want some information as to his existence and evidence of his occupations, which are entirely wanting in your holy book. We cannot worship a name, as the ignorant savages do. We want a god with a character worthy of admiration, and no one has yet shown us such a being in the universe—or in the Bible.

Newton, the world's greatest genius in clear mathematical reasoning, and also in his absolutely mechanical view of matter and motion as the only entities, gave us the tools, and some of his results, to be employed in the solution of the great cosmic problems. There can be no loss nor gain in an infinite universe, and we can imagine no other. We cannot place a boundary, so the system is an infinite one as to time, space, motion, and matter. No boundary can be placed to these entities, so it is a state of things " than which we can imagine no other " or of which the mind " runs not to the contrary." To postulate any boundary to space is to be countered with the question " What is behind your boundary " ? That being an early conclusion of my youth, my thoughts were concentrated on gaining a knowledge of the universe, so I read astronomy, physics, geology and chemistry, and kept touch of the general advance of science, although my useful practical life lay in chemistry and metallurgy. I acquired a moderately good telescope when quite young, so that I could see the things of which I read. Einstein's "curved space " does not help me.

I discovered at an early age the fact that, instead of saying we cannot " grasp infinity," the truth was that we cannot place a boundary to any cosmic matter, whether it is matter, force, time, or space; they elude any boundary. Space is infinite and where there is space there are stars, and larger telescopes simply show us more and more of the universe, and it seems to be peopled with stars, just as it is in our more immediate surroundings. The idea of ether as a conveyer of light was always impossible to me, because, if ether is continuous, light should travel with infinite velocity, hence, I held space to be a true vacuum with some " radiant " entity or particles bringing its tidings from other worlds or suns. The spectroscope at one time seemed to point to light as waves in some medium, but that phase has passed.

If light is composed of particles, as we now suppose, then the bending of light in passing the sun does not require Einstein's crooked mathematics. Its particles are acted upon (as is the earth) by gravitation, but its velocity is so high that the effect is small.

My present picture of the universe is the same as my earliest scientific reasoning—matter and motion in otherwise absolutely empty space (a true vacuum), heat and light being radiant matter in some form, in motion, at a speed of 185,000 miles per second, and perhaps other finer grades of matter at still higher velocities, these particles gradually forming great banks of dust, which we call nebulæ, in which nuclei form and new vortices grow, forming " another and another phase of things for ever," as the Greek philosophers taught. Of course, there are other " accidental " phases, such as direct collisions of suns and grazings or very close passings, breaking up established systems and forming others. One can imagine some such state of affairs, whereas a sudden creation from nothing is unthinkable. So the universe will always be " on the whole " just what it is to-day, in the mass, but with continuous change individually as to suns and planets, etc., with an infinite history, as we cannot place a boundary as to either time or space in the past or future, even with the aid of Einstein's " curved space."

The one element wanted is a workable hypothesis of the mechanism of the force called gravitation. It is the most easily felt and demonstrated of all forces. I have always had a leaning to the idea of a general radiation of particles of very high veolcity from all directions equally, *since space is infinite*, but this radiation, exerting a pressure from all points by its particles, being arrested *after some penetration* into the heavenly bodies. But each body would shield other bodies in the neighbourhood from some of that radiation ; hence, owing to this screening effect, there would be less bombardment from the direction of the intervening body, so two such bodies would be impelled towards each other, instead of " pulled " or " attracted." As we know that we cannot shield off gravitation as we do light or radiant heat, this would necessitate the idea that this " gravitative " radiation or pressure is from a medium very much finer than physical atoms or " electrons," so that it could pass through ordinary matter with much less loss than heat or light, but still would be finally stopped by a large enough mass. This would necessitate the idea of this gravitative bombardment heating the planets or other bodies, and might account for the internal heat, which reaches quite close to the earthly surface and which otherwise ought to have been lost ages ago.

Such an explanation may satisfy our thirst for a theory which seems to "work," until facts hitherto unimagined are in time discovered, and then we get another step towards "reality." Bombardment, which can be to a greater or less extent shielded (cosmic bombardment, equally from all points) is my vision of gravitation, but it may not be a new one, nor a true one.

" When you and I behind the veil are past,
    Oh, but the long, long while this world shall
      last,
    Which of our coming and departure heeds
    As the sea's self should heed a pebble cast."
                                    Omar Khayyám.

APPENDIX

NAMES DERIVED FROM "TSUR"

Tsur is divided into two, Tur and Sur, both meaning "rock"; S becomes Sh; T becomes Th, and the R becomes L.

Sur itself comes from India—Surat, Suraj, Surmah, Suringapatan, and hundreds of Sur names. There are hundreds headed also by Sul, the trisul, triple column, complete male organ of India. So our religion is all Indian.

All the vowels have been used, one replacing the other, so we may tabulate them thus:

Tal	Tel	Til	Tol	Tul	Tyl
Tar	Ter	Tir	Tor	Tur	Tyr

Sar	Ser	Sir	Sor	Sur	Syr
Sarah (Gen. 17, 15)	Seraphim (Isa. 6, 2)	Sirah (2 Sam. 3, 26)	Sorosis	Sur (2 Kings 11, 6)	Syria (Jud. 10, 6)
Sarai (Gen. 17, 15)	Seraiah (2 Sam. 8, 17)	Sirion (Deut. 3, 9)	Sorek (Jud. 16, 4)	Sures	
Sara (Heb. 11, 11)	Serah (Gen. 46, 17)			Suria	
Saron (Acts 9, 35)	Seirath (Jud. 3,26)				
Sargon (Isa. 20, 1)	Seir (Gen. 32, 3)				
Saraph (1 Chron., 4, 22)	Seresh				
Sarahtel					

R and L are the same letter in ancient languages.

Then R is changed to L and we have:

Sal	Sel	Sil	Sol	Sul
Sela (Luke 3, 35)	Selah (2 Kings 14, 7)	Sil	Solomon	Suria
Salah (Gen. 10, 44)	Sela (Isa., 16, 1)	Silla (2 Kings 12, 20)		
Salu (1 Chron. 9, 7)	Seled			
Salai (Neh. 11, 8)				
Salve				
Salamis				
Salathiel				
Salcah				
Salim				
Sallai				
Salmon				
Salome				

S softened into Sh:

Sha	She	Shi	Sho	Shu
Shar	Sheir	Shiloh	Shobal	Shur
Sharia	Sherah	Shiloni	Shoa	Shushan
Sharaim	Sheresh	Shilim	Shobub	Shuthalites
Sharezer	Sherezer	Shilori	Shobach	Shuthelah
Sharon	Sherassur	Shilshah	Shobek	Shulamite
Sharar	Shereph		Shobi	
Shalman	Sheleph		Shoco	
Shalmaneser			Shoham	
Shalmaniah			Shomen	
			Shophach	
			Shophan	

Tyr
Tyre
Tyrus

Zur
Zuriel
Zurnah
Zurishaddai

Tar

Zor
Zorah
Zorah

Tor
Torah
Tola
Tolad
Tolaites

Zil
Zillah

Tir or Til
Timah
Tiria
Tirzah
Tirhannah
Tilon

Ter
Terah
Teresh

Telah

Zer
Zer
Zera
Zeraiah
Zerahiah
Zeri
Zurishadim
Zerah
Zereah
Zeresh
Zereth
Zeruiah
Zeruah
Zerubabal
Zelaph
Zelek
Zelah
Zelek
Zelhal
Zelzah
Zelotes
Zelophehad

Tar or Til
Tarah
Taralah
Tarea
Tarpelites
Tarshish
Tarsus
Tartak
Tartan
Talmon

Zar
Zara
Zarhites
Zareah
Zared
Zareathites
Zarephath
Zaretan
Zartanah
Zarthan
Zalaph
Zareah
Zelab
Zelzah
Zelel

L becomes R. Vowels vary anyhow.

NAMES IN BIBLE: PALA, PUL, PHULLUS (Hindoo for male organ).

(A few of the various words derived from. There are hundreds more.)

Paarl

Palal (the phallus god is Al, Jacob's god)

Palti, the phallus is the god Ti (Chinese)

Palestine (phallus country, Phallus-stan)

Paluites

Pallu, phallu, double-sex

Paltite

Paral (palah), purah, Para

Paruah

Paltiel ("Pul" is the god in Indian language)

Palutite, Para ("Pal" is the god Ti (China) and El (Asia)

Paphos

Para (Pala)

Puram, Palam (double sex)

Parbar

Parnach

Parieh

Parthians

Par-u-ah

Pelaiah (Pel-a, or Pal-a, is Iah, both male and female)

Pelaliah

Pharaoh [Fara-O]

Pharesh

Philip

Philippi

Philistia

Philistine (the phallus country)

Philistines (Phallus-stan)

Phurah (pur-ah, male-female)

Pua, Phurah, Puah

Puah (male-female)

Pul, Pala (male)

Pur, Pala

Purim (Kipurim)

Purah, Phuruh

Pagal (abominable thing)

Pedahzur (the rock is my deliverer)

Pedaiah (whom the Lord has delivered)

Pum, mouth, aperture (pu+m, feminine)

Put, to be, sprout, open

(Pudendum muliebre), secret parts, pulpit, Yomi's own doors

Patash (spread out)

Puten (open the womb)

Pelatiah, Pela-ti-Iah (the double-sexed Pel-a god is double-sexed Iah god) | Pala (set apart, dedicate)
Pala
Penuel, Pen U el (male-female, is god) | Palach
Peniel (Pen, I, El, penis, god) | Pelegesh (concubine)
Persians | Pelaiah, Kadesh, abv.
Persis | Pelach (to cleave, " to bring forth ")
Phalec
Phallu
Phalti, Phaltiel (phallus god, phallus god is El)

MISCELLANEOUS NAMES FROM TSUR

Ts becomes Z and T. Vowels vary anyhow.

Ahishar	Azur	Melzar	Telassar
Asher, Aser	Elasar	Mibzar	Thara
Ashur	Enhazor	Mizar	Trylath pileser
Assurim	Gazer	Na zar eth (enc.)	Tunnall Sorah
Assir	Gashur	Pashur (rozzem)	Sherah
Assyria	Gezer	Seir	Zer
Belshuzzar	Hazar	Shapher	Zerah (many Zer's)
Bethzur	Hazor	Sharon	Zethar
Bezer	Jazer	Shenazar	Zar
Ezer, Ezar	Jasher	Sherah	
Ebenezer	Jesher	Sherezer	
Eleazar	Jetur		
Eliezer	Jether		
Elizur	Joezer		

IAH, HAI, HAI or AI, or AIJA, AIJA

Ezer	Abiezer	Ram	Abram, Abiram
Jah	Elijah	Rahan	Abraham
Shur	Abishur	Salome	Absalom
Ram	Abiram	Addon	Abaddon
Nadab	Abinadab	Ana	Abana
Shallun	Abishalom	El	Abel (father of El)
Shua	Abishua	(Jah), Iah	Abiah
Shur	Abishur	Asaph	Abiasaph
Sephar	Abiasaph		Abib
Eliab	Abiel		Abidah
Ater	Abiathan	El	Abiel
Dan	Abidan	Ezer	Abiezer
El	Abiel	Jah	Abijah
Melech	Abimelech	Melech	Abimelech
Jah	Abijah	Nadab	Abinadab
Melech	Abimelech	Ram	Abiram
Nadab	Abinadab	Shallum	Abshalom
Noam	Abinoam	em	
Ram	Abiram	im	
Shallum	Abishallum	Shua	Abishua
Ner	Abner	Shur	Abishur

A FEW SAMPLES OF THE *ENCYCLOPÆDIA BIBLICA* ADMISSIONS AND CRITISCISM OF BIBLE STATEMENTS

(Amongst hundreds of similar criticisms)

Jesus=Sun God, (*Encyc. Bib.*, col. 3,352, also 3,356, 3,359 and 3,347). Born when the sun is born, crucified when the sun crosses, and ascends to Heaven summer (3,291), and the Salvation of Mankind. Jesus, born at Bethlehem, city of David, to please orthodox Jews, and at Galilee for sun-god circle of the year, 12 months (*Encyc. Bib.*, 3,347).

Names.

Artless attempts (3,271)

Much remains obscure (3,272)

Hebrew imperfectly known (3,272)

Names chosen arbitrarily (3,272)

Hebrew unvocalised, never spoken nor pronounced (3,272)

Knowledge of Hebrew very imperfect (3,274)

Meaning often unintelligible (3,274)

Interpretation barely possible (3,274)

Explanations merely tentative (3,274)

Fictitious character of the list plainly shows itself (3,274)

[this refers to Gen. 10, 13, 14 (Ludim, father in stones, loins, etc.) (3,274) intensely phallic passage repeated I Chron. 1, 11-12]

Nativity.

Two accounts, Matthew and Luke, are irreconcilably at variance (3,340)

Mutually exclusive and irreconcilable (3,343)

Quite different structures (3,343)

Gospels make Joseph the descendant of David (not Mary), but Joseph had nothing to do with the parentage of Jesus

Gospels know nothing of the miraculous birth of our Saviour (3,344)

[Before they had come together]

Absolute incompatibility between the narratives of the nativity and these genealogies, of which Joseph, *not Mary*, is the subject

No son of Joseph

Verse 18, " When his mother was espoused to Joseph, before they came together she was found to be with child of the Holy Ghost

Matt., I, 25, " And he knew her not till she had brought forth her first-born son, and called his name Jesus "

Names in Old Testament must be regarded as fictitious (3,275)

Invented to fill gaps (3,275)

Mythical patriarchs down to Abraham (3,275)

Exact measurements of Noah's Ark and other impossible statistics as to the numbers of the Israelite tribes (3,275)

Some of these personages had no existence (3,275)

Names coined by the prophets (3,276)

INDEX

A

Aaron made Israelites naked to their shame, 97

Abraham's wife and sister a god (*Encyc. Bib.*), 112-113

Abraham's oath on " thigh," 122

Acropolis or Polacra, Phalacra, 100

Adam, red thing, 35

Adamah, Eve, the female red thing, 35

Adam and Eve mean the male and female red things, 35

Aleph, א, rod and serpent, or god-serpent, 124

Alexandrian collection of religions, 2, 3

All Bible names artificial concoctions, 133, 165

Allah's Lat, phallus, 36, 37

All churches founded on harlotry, hence phallic nomenclature, 108, 110

All Church's income from prostitution, 110

All gods double-sexed, 61

All Church paraphernalia double-sexed, 61

All kings, apostles, saints, gods and godesses had double-sex names, 61

All Bible names fictitious, 79

All Bible writings declared to be pseudepigrapha, " sham writings " (*Encyc. Bib.*), 110

All holy things double-sexed, 5

" Almond-shaped " monstrance, 121-122

All names have meanings, 80-81

All names in Bible symbolical creations, 166-168

All names founded on double-sex, 68

All nations pray to their gods in the form of double-sexed symbols—pillar, bowl, or capital, lingam-yoni altar, idol, icon, IO three in one, IHH in O, all indicating coition, 161-164

All religious names based on double-sex, 60, 61

All religions phallic, 65-69

All " revealed " faiths must die out, 186

All symbolism arose from sex organs, 109-110

Almond letter O, 9

Almond or dove-shaped vessel, woman, 122

Almond, favourite symbol for woman, 105

Almond, yoni, woman's organ, 92

Alphabet (new), meaning of letters hidden, 9

Altar is " Maha Devâ," great god, 67

Ancient god ideas, all phallic, worshipped as creators, 33

Anointing and " washing feet," 57-58

Aph and Eph mean serpent (in names), 113, 114

Ararat, Allah's Lat, 36–37

Arah's Rat, Ararat, 36, 37

Ark, and monstrance and pyx (Aron), 139

Ardha-Nari Eswara, 156, 184

Ark, Aron, Alon, double-sexed, 139

Ark, 28–36

Ark of Tabernacle, death to touch, 10

Ark and Tabernacle fictitious, 28

Ark abandoned, 139

Ark of Covenant, woman, 123

Ark story, woman's gestation, 37

Arnobius anointed stones everywhere, 77

Arnobius begged blessing from anointed stones, 78

Artificial sex-organ god names in Bible, 1

Asoka's Lat, pillar or phallus, 36

Asoka, Ptolemy Soter, and Rome, 23

Aspirate H, " breath of life " letter, 9

Augustine, St., clean linen, " holy kiss " administered, 56–106

Author's studies, 155

B

Baal, Bamoth, stinking gods of the pulpits (double-sex chambers for prostitution), 136–137

Baal, equivalent to mortar and pestle, or pulpit, 136–137

Baal, baah, to swell out, 136

Baal, Basar, Osiris or Min, 136

Babylonians, brute strength, 151

Baby's first cry, Ma, universal female symbol, 13

Babylonians lashing Hebrew slaves, 21

Bam, Bom, Bum, Bamah, Bamoth, Behemoth, all phallic, 136

Behemoth, 133

Barbaric (scriptures), sacred documents, 3

Beisan in Palestine, Egyptian occupation of, 86

Beauty evenings, 40

Bell, double-sexed god (mortar and pestle), 164

Bible criticism, 154

Bible a growth of centuries under Romans, 207

Bible a necessity for Roman government, 31

Biblical rod of god and two stones, 76

Bible (Roman) caused " dark ages," 20

Bible a gigantic fraud, a political engine, 166

Bible a pure " pen product," 166–168

Bible names from phallic roots, 5

Bible gods Elohim, plural, 10

Bible made up of pseudepigrapha, " sham writings " (Encyc. Bib., col. 3,525), 110

Bible writing took centuries, 4

Bible and confessional (two diabolical engines), 31

Bible for clergy only, 32

Bible in unreadable text, 32

Bible phallic throughout, but not one person in a thousand in England knows the meaning of " phallic," 69

Bible an invention of the Romans, 25

Bible shamelessly immoral book (Mrs. Grundy), 111

Bible declares that Jerusalem was never held by Hebrews or Jews, who never were a nation, 87

Bible names from phallic roots, 5

Bible obscure (*Encyc. Bib.*), 4-5

Bible names from phallic roots, 111

Bible entirely fictitious, Church professors know that, 111

Bible secret (not for laity, unreadable), 31

Bible written between 150 A.D. and 690 A.D., 19

Bible to end wars, 2

Bible names from Indian pala and other phallic words, 5

Bible folk-lore, fables, phallic, 33

Bible story artificial, not real, 4, 166

Bible to hold people in subjection, 166

Bible gigantic fraud, vast imposture, 166

Bible made by Romans for government, 111

Bible Hebrew a mere sequence of symbolical letters (*Encyc. Bib.*), 25

Bible gods mere letter symbols (*Encyc. Bib.*), 25

Bible meaning often unintelligible (*Encyc. Bib.*), 26

Bible Hebrew never spoken (*Encyc. Bib.*), 26

Bible entirely fictitious " sham writings " (*Encyc. Bib.*), 110

Biblical criticism, all Bible destroyed by, 110

Bible contradicts its own statements, 21-22

Bible names fictitious (*Encyc. Bib.*), 4

Bible imposed on us by the Romans, 79

Bible, issue of, 188, 199

Birdwood, Oman, Burton, Johnston, gave many accounts of phallism, 78

Bishops had harems, one had 70 children, 104

Bishop of Liége had 70 children, 104

Blasphemy, 18

" Blasphemy " of translators, 19

Blasphemy means " to speak to the hurt of anyone," 18

Blind to dangerous texts, clergy, 110, 111

Bom, pulpit, " high place," brothel, 80

Book or Bible, inception of, 31

Bible, inception of, 31

Brazen serpent, 107, 108

Brazen serpent, Aleph, god serpent, alphabet " house of the god serpent " (reading was priests' refuge), 124

Brazen serpent raised by Moses, 123, 124

Breath-of-life letter H, two egg founts of life, 120

Breath-of-life letter, testes, 120

Breath-of-life letter H, aspirate, 9

British false pronunciation, 167

British phallic feasts, 99

Brucium Library burnt down, 47 B.C., 3

Burton, Sir Richard, on phallism, 78

C

Cæsars claimed to be gods, and they were believed, 88

Cato on Rome's orgies, sex festivals, 39

Cato, pornographic feasts in all savage nations, 39

Catholic, Kata and Holos, universal, 33

Christians had private prostitution, no fees to pay, 106

Christos copied from Christna, 146

Christna 800 years before Christ, 146

Christos and Christna, names of identical meaning, 23, 131

" Christ " does not arise from krio, 145

Christna and Christ, identical incidents in lives of, 145-146

Christos, fish sign, miracles, 148-150

Christos and Christna, names of identical meaning, 147-8-9, 150

Christos and Christna identical in meaning, 145

Christos and Christna data identical, 147-150

Christ is pronounced Kreist by our parsons to keep us from guessing Christna. They don't say Kreistians, but Kristians or Christians, 132

Christos is a strongly double-sexed word, 131

Christna, male-female creative god, 131

Christ and Christna, data of events identical, 132, 144, 147-149, 169-179

Christianity the same as paganism, 44

Christian era, Galilee, 19

Christian religion combination of phallism and sun-worship, 160

Christna and Christos both sun-gods, 145

Christians destroyed priests' revenues from prostitution, as they were " free lovers," 106

Church architecture all phallic, sex organs mean eternal life, phallism is the basis of things and words in all religions

from China to Peru, Persian Yima's piercer and ring; marriage in French is " husbanded," 69-70

" Charms " in Italy, Tiber, Seine and Thames, 48

Children saw sex orgies (Rome), 39

Children's fêtes ought to be encouraged, 100

Children witness phallic orgies, 39-42

Children listen to libidinous songs and laugh, 42, 43

Churches were brothels, 108, 109, 110

Church revenues entirely from prostitution, 57, 94

Clay tablets of cuneiform in Palestine, 19

Cement of universal religion, 77

Colenso secured mental freedom for us, 20

Colenso (biblical scholars' St. George), 20

Colenso, St. George of religion, 20

Colenso defeated persecutors, 20

Colenso set men free from Jesuitical lying control, 20

Colenso, 20

Colenso on Exodus, 22

Colenso on Hebrew exaggerations, 22-23

Colenso on Crosses, 75

Cleopatra last of Ptolemy's line, 3

Christianity, same as paganism, 44

Church income derived entirely from prostitution, 57

Circumcision abandoned, 187

Circumcision in Britain, 60

Corinth and Eryx, 43

Columns, phallus, and two stones, testes, symbols of life producers, 212

Concubitus Œdipei, 44

Cobra in Egypt shows Indian origin of Egyptian symbolism, 124

Coition sacred act even by prostitutes, 64

Confessional, Rome's secret engine, 31

College of priests to create Bible at Galilee, 4

College of learned men at Galilee, 4

Constructed a sort of language, never spoken, 132

Concealment of Bible making at Constantinople, 208

Conclusion: The author's opinion of the Christian Bible, 215

Corruptions of pala, pel, pul, phyl, etc., 61–62

Consecrated women, 137–138

Condemnation of Bible by *Encyc. Bib.*, as fictitious, 26

Columba dove Iona, 67-68

Common-sense translation would ruin the Church's business, 111

College of Romans at Galilee, 4

Consecrated women white slaves, as they brought in the temple revenues, 137–138

" Creative " religion phallic, 5

Creative god, 96, 128

Creative religion, sex organs, 5

Creation of Hebrew, 132

Creation needs two sexes, 6

Creators named naturally from the two creative organs, no other method of naming conceivable, 61

Creative religion, double sex, 6

Creative or phallic names, male organ, 6

Creative words phallic, 6

Critics of Oxford shut their eyes to phallism, 110, 111

Cross is phallic, complete male organ, phallus with testes, 70, 71

Crosses, Colenso, 75

Cross worshipped by cave-men, 74–75

Crossing places, 75

Cross, complete male organ, rod of god and two stones, 122

Cross from " crossing " places, 75, 76

Cubicles 8ft. × 5ft. for concubinage in temple, 45, 46

Cubicles called Lesakoth, " being joined," also interchange of liquids or mixture of liquids, things which pour out, 46, 48

Cubicles for prostitution in all temples, 45, 46

Cunningham Graham, " women here all amateurs, so brothel would yield no profit," 44

" Custom of women is upon me," Rachel, 125

Cuneiform in Palestine, 15

D

Dad, 133

Dagger and ring create life, 70

Dangerous texts avoided by critics, 110, 111

David, red thing, 36

Death penalty for trying to understand priests' phallic symbols, 121, 122

Dagger and ring, 8

Dayanand, 62

Dead Osiris, women chafing phallus, 142, 143

Death penalties for touching holy things or pronouncing holy name, 7–8

Death to pronounce holy name, 6–10

" Deadly sin " is doubt, 185

Death to touch holy things, 10

Debir, little cells for prostitution, 46

Derivations of Tsur, Sul, etc., 115

Deus, Dio, Dios, Theos, Ti, Di, 8

Diana, new moon, 35

Dishonesty of Protestants, 18

Dr. Angus Smith, cromlechs, two stones, 140

Di, De, Ti, the god particles from China, 8

Dome of church, d'om, place of the womb, 123

Dolphin skins, 123

Door of life, 9

Door of life, O, U and V, female, 9

Dorchester pillar, 72

Dorset pillar, " Lost pyx," 122

Double-sex, sacred, so all Church furniture, etc., was double-sexed, 60–61

Double-sex names in all Church paraphernalia and structures (list), 102–103

Double-sexed Hindoo altars, 65, 67

Double sex necessary for creation, 61

Doubled-sexed life produces IO, 9

Double-sexed gods, Elohim, 10

Doubt is the deadly sin (in Church), 185

E

Each writer in *Encyc. Bib.* criticized part, till all is destroyed as authority, 110

Eastern sources of Bible literature (Di and Ti, Chinese roots of " divine " theology), etc., 204

Encyc. Bib., names fictitious, 81

Ee-oo-no, IUNO, 13

Egg in Latin and Greek, 120, 121

Egypt held Palestine always, 86

Egyptian palaces in Palestine, at Beisan, 86

Egyptian palaces on both sides of the Jordan right up to Beisan, gateway to Tyre, 152

Egg in Greek, Oon, so N is part of female, like M, 96–97

Egg, ovum, etc., feminine, 97

Egyptian phallic pillars, 163–164

Egyptian occupation of Palestine, 86

Egyptian occupation of Beisan, 15, 16

Egyptian buildings in Palestine, 15

Egyptian palaces and barracks in Palestine, 16

Egypt always held Palestine, 86, 87

Eli, god, Elohim gods, 10

Emperors were Sons of God, 88

Elohim, double-sexed band of gods, translated " God " in Bible, 10

Elohim, dishonest translation, 10

Encyc. Bib. on religious prostitution, 78–81

Encyc. Bib. says Epistles are pseudepigrapha, " sham writings," 110

Encyc. Bib. on Sarah, 112, 113

Encyc. Bib. says Bible " mythical " and impossible, 165, 166

Encyc. Bib. shows Bible an imposture, 165, 166

Encyc. Bib. names, 4

Encyc. Bib. criticisms of Bible, 165–166

Encyc. Bib. names' true meaning fatal to Bible, 4–5

English fraud to hide symbolism, 23, 24

English pronunciation all wrong, 128

English J unknown in other languages, 18, 19

Entire revenue of priests came from prostitution, 94

Eryx and Corinth prostitution, 43

Eternal life through Bible, Rome's bribe, 2

English corrupt foreign names, 65

English "sex-shy," 69

Es, "flesh," Hindoo particle, 161

Everlasting life, double sex, 111

Ephods, double-sexed articles, serpent and testicle, 164

Equinoctial feasts, Hags, 98

Eswara, Guardian of the Flesh, 168

"Es." Flesh, with IU, double-sex god IesU, "god in the flesh," 47, 167

Eternal succession of life, 1, 111

Eunuchs proved that "stones" necessary to life production, 9–10

Eunuchs infertile, wanting testes, 120

Ex-communication, Rome's terrible power, 30

English reticence on sex-religion, even "sex" is barred in conversation, 69

F

Fables of Osiris, 167

Fair-Oh instead of Fârâ-oh, two syllables instead of three, 65

Fellah, fellow, 37

Female organ, yoni, ee-on-ee, all I's like double E, 64

Feet, hair symbolism, 57—58

Fictitious statements, Encyc. Bib. does not tell us how they arose, 28

Fictitious character of Bible known to Church professors, 26, 109, 110, 111

"Filthy sensuality" condemned by modern Church, by Encyc. Bib., was the Roman Church's sole source of income, 108, 109–110

Finished Bible, 197–198

Flood, history of woman's gestation, 126

Flood phallic, 37

Flood story, 125

Forlong's greatest work, 78

Forlong, Major-General, great work on phallism, 78

Formation of the Bible texts and stories, feet and hair, 188–190

Four hundred years to produce Bible, 202

Four-letter name, Lord, IHOH. 10

Free Kadeshoth Christians, 106

G

Galilee religion of solar circle, 6–7

Galilee (Tyberya), 6

Galilee circle of year, 6

Galilee, circle of year, sun-worship, 7

Galilee, circle of year, 196

Galilee on lake of Tyberya, 4

Garden of Eden story, 114

Gemini, twin pillars, 209

General view of word making, 95–97

God, 9–10

God, 3-letter word Eli, 10

God, made flesh for us 12 times, 7

God and Lord in Bible, 10

God-names derived from Tsur, 81

Gods, goddesses, saints, kings, double-sexed, 46, 47
God idea, two sexes in one individual (hermaphroditic), 6
God is love, IU, IO, etc., 19
God made flesh for us 12 times in Epistles, 168, 169
"God made flesh for us," 157
God named from two sexes, 60–61
Gods, double-sexed band of, 9–10
Gold and silver in thousands of tons, Solomon, 20
Great God, "Maha Devâ," sex organs, 69
God name invented by Romans between 150 A.D. and 690 A.D., 19
God-serpent, Aleph, 124
God-serpent House, Al-Eph-Beth = Alphabet, 124
Gods, patriarchs, kings, prophets are phallic, 7–10
Gravitation, 223
Greeks corrupted languages, 89
Greek Φ, philip, phyllis, etc., love, 89
Growth of a "universal religion" idea, bettering this life, 186

H

H, breath-of-life letter, 120
H, breath-of-life letter, at each side of O, 120
H, breath-of-life letter, stones, 9—10
H may also mean ovaries, 120
H, male and female testes, ovaries, 120
H represented breath of life, or stones, 9–10
H, stones, breath of life, 9—10
H, I, O, U, V, secret, sacred letters, 9

"Hag," of Uapés, 41
Hag, phallic orgy, 41, 98
Hag, ate, drank, made merry, 98
Happiness through Bible, Rome's bribe, 2
Hair symbolism, 58
Hardy's "Lost Pyx," 71, 72
Hardy's pillar, 71
Hebrew not a living language, 25
Hebrew, bastard language for universal religion, 86–87
Hebrews a Roman myth, 204
Hebrew, a priests' language like Zend of Persia, 132
Hebrew an invention of Romans, 59
Hebrew alphabet invented to conceal meanings of letters, 9
Hebrew alphabet, secret, 13, 14
Hebrew artificial, 26, 27
Hebrew invented to hide meaning, 11, 12
Hebrew names invented, 27
Hebrew, "new secret" alphabet and language, 8–9
Hebrews worshipped Jebusites' gods, 87
Hebrew, none in Palestine, 15
Hebrew, impossible as a daily speech, 26
Hebrew never spoken, 25
Hebrew verbs, 800 inflexions, 25
Hebrew merely a sequence of letters, 25
Hebrew never spoken, 26
Hebrew could not be pronounced nor spoken (Encyc. Bib.), 26
Hebrew, phantom race, 22
Hebrews only slaves, 22
Hebrew meaning unintelligible (Encyc. Bib.), 27
Hebrew complicated, 27
Hebrew no language, only symbols for religion, 25
Hebrew, none in Palestine, 123
Hebrew impossible as a daily language, 26

Hebrew sprang from theoretical rules and symbolical letters, 25

Hebrew, Rome's secret alphabet, 12, 13, 14

Hebrew, disguised phallic meanings, 14

Hebrews were always slaves, 22

Hebrews boasting of wealth, 22-23

Hebrew words or letters, none in Palestine, 15

Hebrew neither pronounced nor spoken (*Encyc. Bib.*),24, 25, 26

Hebrew names invented (*Encyc. Bib.*), 27

Hebrew had not a natural growth, 26

Hebrew can be translated in many ways (*Encyc. Bib.*), 27

Hebrew took 400 years to be invented, 27

Hebrew kingdom a myth, 86, 87

Hebrew patriarchs mythical, 27

Hebrew, how it arose, 27, 28

Hebrews did *not* hold Palestine, (Judges III, 5), 21, 22

Hebrew impossible of being spoken, 24, 25

Hebrew cannot be spoken, 132

Hebrews' 5,848 tons of gold, 22, 23

Hebrew unvocalised (*Encyc. Bib.*), 32

Hebrew often unintelligible, 26, 27

H's, two breath-of-life stones, 9, 10

Hermes, the lively god, 6

Herodotus found no Palestine, 19

Hermaphroditic or Omphallic, 119

Hermes (Mercury) and Aphrodite (Venus), to produce life, 6

Hermaphroditic or Omphallic, 6

Hermaphroditic ideas, double-sex, 6

Hermaphrodites, all gods, 6

Hermaphrodites, two sexes necessary to create life, 6

Hardy's column, Dorchester, 72

Hundreds of thousands all over the world, 72

Harlotry chief source of wealth to priests, 103-104

Hieroglyphics phallic, 64

Hindoo symbolism in Bible, 168

Hermaphroditic words, 6

Hindoo fables in Bible, 1

Hundreds of phallic columns in Britain, 90

" High place," brothel, 45, 80

Holy Book necessary, 30-31

Holy kiss, clean linen, St. Augustine, 44

H, breath-of-life aspirate, 9

Holi festival, children saw obscenities, 42

HOH, Eve, woman and ovaries, a goddess, 141

" Holiness," 5

Holy oil called " semen " (Latin for seed), 77

Holiness of prostitutes, Kadeshoth, 55

Hogmanay, in Scotland, 98-99

HOH=Eve, or womb and ovaries, 141

Hogmanay, 98

Holy four letters, tetragrammaton, IHOH, 7

" Holy kiss," clean linen for Eucharist love feast, 56

I

I represents phallus, or rod of God, in Roman letters, 138-139

Israelites always under-dogs and slaves, 22

I made into J to hide meaning, 9

Identical incidents, Christ and Christna (list only), 147, 148, 149; ditto with full references, 169-179

I disguised as J, 17-18

I's dishonestly made into J's in our Bible, 128

I represented by a comma, 14

I, pillar, represents male, 11, 12

Identical incidents in lives of Christna and Christ, 169-179

Iah common in Bible names, 144-5

Iah a double-sexed god, 144

IHOH sacred, death to pronounce it, 111

IHOH unpronounceable, 10, 119

IHOH, meaning of, 9

IHOH life-creating combination (symbol), 111

IHOH unutterably sacred, 111

IHOH, curse on those without "stones," 120

IHOH too sacred name, Adonai substituted, 121

IHOH stones, breath of life, 120

IHOH, IesU unknown, 19

IHOH, IHUH, IHVH, 10

IHOH, IHUH, or IHVH, 127

IHOH same as ark, rod, and stones, 138-139

IHOH Jehovah, 10

IHOH in Hebrew, 11

IHOH unpronounceable, 119

IHOH, IesU, 16

IHOH, 5-6, 7-8

I, O, U, V, symbols, 11

IHOH (to pronounce was death), 7, 8

IHOH, death to question, 7-8

IHOH in Hebrew, 11

IHOH, ineffable four letters, 10

Immoral stories, 14-15

Images, 113, 114

IHS, Iesu Hominum Salvator, 24

I disguised, 14

Iesu Hominum Salvator, 24

Iesu disguised as our Jesus, 2-3

Iesu or Jesus, 2-3

Iesu, explanation of name, Encyc. Bib. erroneous, 156, 157, 158

Iesu, IU, IHOH, 156

Iesu, descent to earth, "god made flesh," life same as all solar gods, 158

IesU in all countries except English-speaking, 23, 24

IesU, "Es," flesh, IU god or spirit creator, double-sex, 160, 161

IesU, new god Yaisoo, 23, 24

Iesu Christos, Yaisoo Kreestos, 144

IesU, 19

IU, double-sex god surrounding Es, flesh, god in the flesh, IesU, 167-168

Iesu Christna, erroneously Jesus Christ, 23

IO, IU or IV, god symbols, 12-13

IU, IUNO, IHUH, IU-piter, IesU, 19

I, O, U, V, symbols, 9

IO, 9

IO, male and female life producer, 9

IO, rendered JO in Bible, 9

IO in Joseph, 114, 119

IO, Greek Φ, IU, IV, 12

Isaiah = Eesa-Yah (or Iah), 144-145

I, pillar, male organ, pala, 8-9

IUNO, three times female, 13-14

IUno, Juno, 19

IUpiter, Jupiter, 19

IVNO, correctly IUNO, 13

IU instead of Jew, 18

IUpiter, J for I dishonestly, 128

IU, rod and almond, 9, 94

Indian Ling, Lingah, Lingam, 64

Israelites under Jebusites in Jerusalem, 21–22

I, pillar letter, phallus, 9

Isis, Serapis, added "is" to names, 89

IO, dagger and ring, life producer, 9

IO is printed JO in Bible to conceal phallic meaning, 9

IHOH, double-sex creative god, 7

Issue of Bible, 198, 199

IOseph, Joseph, 114

I, O, U, V, in symbolism, 127

IOseph (Joseph), Garden of Eden story, 11

Kings' god-mark, 12

Isaiah, Messiah, 145

Isaiah should be "Eeså-yah," 145

English terrible mispronouncers, 64–65

Iona, 67–68

Ireland, nude sculpture over church doors, 34

Images, 113

Isra El, 78–79

Israelites under the lash, 21

Imposition of Bible by Romans, 1

Italian superstition, 38

IHOH, Jehovah, 118, 119

IHOH, erroneously translated Jehovah, 7–8

IHOH, double-sex, creative letters, 5–6

IO and IAH identical male and female particles, 160, 161

IHOH, Holy Tetragrammaton, 7

Iesu Christos, 144

IHOH, holy name, death to pronounce, 7–8

IesU, Yaizu, 56

Ineffable IHOH, 121

Income of temples entirely from prostitution, 110

R

J

J for I, capital disguise of phallism, 204–205

J instead of I to hide symbolism, 10, 18–19

Jakin and Boaz, 162

Jacob's pillar, 78

Jacob worships the virgo intacta, 54–56

Jack and Jill, 137

Jehovah, IHOH, IHUH, or IHVH, 127

Jehovah, Herr, Dieu, 8

Jehovah, IHOH, 7, 8

Jehovah, IHOH, pronounciation quite wrong, 7, 8

Jeremiah, rod and almond, 105–106

J in place of I in names, a good disguise for phallism, 204, 205

J's in Bible all fraudulent, 23–24

Jacob, "This is El, god of Israel," 78

J for I, dishonest change, 18

Jesus in mortal flesh, 156, 158

Jesus, or Iesu, Yesu, 23

Jesus, correctly Iesu, Yaisoo, 23

Jesus is IesU, god in the flesh, Christ a Hindoo saviour, 168

Jesus has become similar to IHOH, Jehovah, 111, 112

"Jesus" means man clothed with spirit of god, 167

Jesus feebly rebukes sale of doves, prostitutes in open temple instead of in the cubicles, 56

Jew, fraudulent name, 18

Jew, a word to veil IU, symbol of double-sex, 18

Jew is simply IU, 18

J for I, fraud or ignorance ?, 204

Jeremiah I, 11, "Rod and almond," 93–94

JO used to conceal meaning of IO, 9

Job's god playing, "sporting," 134

Job's Leviathan and Behemoth, phallic, 134-136

Job's phallic god, 134

Johnston, Sir Harry, on phallism, 78

Joseph should be IOseph, 128

Joseph, IOseph, 11

Joseph should be Yoseph, as even lady novelists know, 128

Julius Cæsar and Cleopatra, 3

Julius Cæsar, son of a god ! ! !, 88

Juno, Iuno, 12, 13

Juno, IUno, 19

Jupiter, IUpiter, 19

Jurapari, worship of, by Uapés, 41

K

Kadeshim, male prostitutes, 105, 106

Kadeshoth and Kadeshim, male and female prostitutes, 93, 105

Kadeshim and Kadeshoth, male and female prostitutes, 55, 105

Kadeshoth, nuns, fish, sun in Pisces, 94, 95

Kings made gods on coronation, 12

Kings' god-mark, broad arrow, 12

Kristna or Christna, Christos, 23

L

Leaping and playing, naked Israelites, 57

L and R replace one another, 36, 37

Lad, lat (T and D same letter), 36, 37

Ladder to heaven, virgo intacta, 54-55

Ladies to wear clean linen as the holy kiss was administered, 56

Lake Tyberya or Tuberia, 6

Learned writers missed essential point, 110-111

Lecky on European morals, 104

Lecky, morality unknown, 104

Lesakoth, small chambers for prostitution in temples, 46

Lecky's "History of European Morals," 44

Lecky on European morals, 44

Lake Tyberya called Galilee by Romans, 6

Letters of Holy (four) Tetra-grammaton, 7

Letter I represents the phallus in Roman alphabet, 9

Lesakoth, little chambers for prostitution, 57

Leviathan and Lord, IHOH, smoke, sparks and flame from mouth, 135

Liberalia, Floralia, etc., one for each month, 38

Liberalia (list of feasts), 38

Life-creating property of a god IHOH, 119-120

Linen clean for holy kiss, Augustine, 56

Lingam-Yoni altars, several, 182-3-4

Lists illustrating creation of Bible names, Appendix

Lingam-Yoni altar, popular in India, 66

Lingam-Yoni (ee-on-ee), 64

List of Encyc. Bib.'s condemnations of Bible, 26, 27

Lord, 4-letter word, IHOH, 9-10

Lord and God in Bible, 7-8

Lovers' towers or keeps, almonds, 94-95

Lucian, "Syrian Goddess," 46

L.Y. altar, 2-sex members represent Maha Devâ, great god, 66

M

Ma, female, baby's first cry, 13

M and N, female symbols, 129–132

M and N in symbolism, 13

Mace from maté, 84–85

Magdalene, 193

Magdala, Magdalene, 105

Male and female (Moses), 121–122

Male and female letters for symbols, 129–130

Male I and female O, creative conjunction, 111

Mari, "she who urges the god to action," 200

Maypole, pretty scene, 100

Marriage, passing finger into ring, male into female, 70

Maidens tearing their hair and chafing Osiris' phallus, 142, 143

Maidens (naked) and serpents, 108

Maidens for great feast, 104

Maidens going up hill for water, 137

Mary chose better part, to support the priests by prostitution, Martha modern idea of goodness, 57

M and N, nasal breathing letters, 129–130

Male and female letters, I, O, U, V, 127

Male and female prostitutes sacred in the Bible, 56, 57

Massekah and Pesselim, 48

Mary Magdalene, temple prostitute, 92, 93

Mary Magdalene, 200

"Mary hath chosen the better part" as far as the priests' salaries went, Mary and Martha, 57–58

Meaning of IHOH, 7–8

Massekah and Pesselim, mortar and pestle, 47 (Fig. 5)

Maté, 85

Maypole girls in wood all night, 99–100

Matthew from Maté, rock of god, 85

"Massekah and Pesselim," 47

Mercury and Venus, double-sex, 6

Messiah, son of Iah, 145

Messiah, Mess Yah, 145

Method of name-making, 5

Migdal Nunia, "keep" for nuns for priests' use, 94–95

Migdal nunya, almonds, nuns or fish, 95

Migdal, Greek for almond, Magdalene, temple prostitute, loved much, 92

Minoa, Min, ithyphallic O Min O, 116–117

Min, 133

"Min," Brit. Mus., 116A

Minoans, double-sexed bull, 209–211

Miraculous story of Bible creation, 15

Minoan double-axe, phallic, 116

Min, ithyphallic, 211, 212

Minoan serpent goddess, 117, 212

Minoans, serpent goddess, large breasts, 209–211

Miracles "childish," *Encyc. Bib.*, 186, 187

Mispronunciation of vowels in English, 128, 129

"Molten images," 47

Monstrance and pyx, 121, 122

Monstrance, pyx, almond and pala, 122

Monstrance and pyx holy (death to touch), 10

Morality as we know it, unknown in Roman times, 33–34

Mortar and pestle, pour out, mix, pesel, 47

Moses, rod of god, 77

Moses, 2 stones, " holy " stones (*Encyc. Bib.*), 77

Moses, 2 stones, not tables of law (*Encyc. Bib.*), 77

Mythical history of Bible, 1

N

NA, NO, OS, US, female, 145

N frequently used for female M, 129, 130

Naked maidens feed serpents, 108

Naked Israelites leaping and playing, 57

Naked phallic feasts universal, 39, 40

Names of sex organs in Bible, 1

Names and stories mutually fictitious, 79

Names from Tsur, 112

Names fictitious, 27

Names Christna, Christos, female termination, both double-sex, 159

Names in Bible all derived from sex-organs, 111

Names of places from Pala, 97

Names of all gods and god symbols, 5

Name making (method of), 4

Names, true meaning fatal to Bible, 5–6

Names all symbolical (*Encyc. Bib.*), 5

Names invented (*Encyc. Bib.*), 26

Names all double-sexed or creative, 4–5

Names in Bible phallic, 5

Names chosen arbitrarily (*Encyc. Bib.*, 3,272), 5

Naturalistic superstition in Bible, 1

Names dervied from Tzur, 81

Nések (M and N equally feminine), root of Massekah, 50

New alphabet hid meanings of letters, 9

New alphabet, 1

New religion phallic, 6

New signs for O, U, V, staff, 14

New moon, Diana, 34–35

New religion in phallic roots, 7

New Testament names, Iesu, 144

Ninevites, strong barbarian, 151

Ninevite plaques show Israelites as slaves, 21

Noah's Flood story means period of gestation and birth, in women, 126

" No Epistle of Paul," founded on a foundation not of rock but of shifting sand (*Encyc. Bib.*, 1,625–1,636), 58–59

No creation without double-sex, 60–61

No Epistle of Paul (*Encyc. Bib.*), 187–188

No Hebrews in Palestine, 85–86

Not one letter of Hebrew in Palestine, 3, 15–16, 85, 86

Not a word about the 300 years' labours, 199

Number 12 in religion, 7

Nothing told of Bible contents of the Mary Magdalenes, white slaves, 193

Number 12 indicates a sun god, 12 months, 12 signs of Zodiac, 12, 168

Isis and Osiris, 167

Nuns, sacred prostitutes, 15

Nude women over church doors, 34

Nunya, female companions (concubines) for priest translators 94, 95

O

O, almond or ring, female member, 8
O represents woman or womb in Roman alphabet, 12
O, U and V abolished in Hebrew alphabet, 14
O, U and V replaced by staff to hide symbolism, 14
O, U and V symbolise the fount of life, 9
O, U, V female, 12
O, U and V same meaning, 9
Œcumenical Councils gave not a whisper of the system of sex symbolism they were evolving, 202
Œcumenical Councils, whole habitable world Catholic, 199
Œdipus Rex, 44, 45
Om, womb, woman, 66, 67
Omphalé, double sex, (om woman, phalé the phallus), 6
Omphale hermaphrodité, 6
Omphale, Hermes and Aphrodité, 6
O.T. prostitution, 45
Omar Kayyám repudiates sun-god, 184
Oman, Dr. J. Campbell on phallism, 78
Oman, Hindoo wedding, 42, 43
Oman, phallic orgies, 42, 43
Oman, children listen to incestuous songs and join in, 42, 43
Oman, Agapæ, 41, 42
Oman, Dr., Agapæ, 42
Omphalé, Om womb and phallos male organ, double-sex, 6
Oman's account of Hindoo songs at marriage, 42, 43
On, like Om, is female, 65
"On," like "Om," is female, 64-65
Onyx, female-male, 96
Opal, double-sex, 95

Opal in names of towns (list) 96
Opal in town names, 95
Oiling stones at every turn in India, Birdwood and Oman, 77, 78
Os, female particle, 132
Osiris, ithyphallic, 167
Osiris, fable of, 167
Ovaries, St. Mary's Cathedral, 120, 121
Ovaries and testes (" stones "), 120, 121
Ovum, ova, all female letters, 120
Ovaries, 140
O, almond ring, female member, 9
O represents woman or womb in Roman alphabet, 12
Œdipus Rex, 44
Oiling stones at every turn in India, 77, 78
Om, womb, woman, 65
Oman's account of Hindoo songs at marriages, 42-43
Oman, Dr. J. Campbell, on phallism, 78
Omphalé, om, womb, phalé, male organ, 6
Omphalé or hermaphrodité, 6
Oman, Hindoo wedding, children listen to incestuous songs, 43
Omar Kayyám repudiates sun-god, 184
Onyx, on, or om, womb, and x, the phallus, double-sex, 96
Opal in names of towns, 95-96
Opal, double-sex, 95-96
Opal (name in towns), list, 96
O, ring of Persia in Yima's creation, 9
Osiris, fable of, 167
Ovaries, St. Mary of, Cathedral, 121
Old Testament prostitution, 45, 46

O, U and V, fount of life, 9
O, U and V, female, 9, 97
O, U and V abolished, 13
O, U and V door of life, 8-10
Osiris, ithyphallic, 166-167
O, U and V, replaced by a rod or staff, 14
O, U and V represent female, 12
Ovum, ova, all female symbols, ova plural, 96, 97
Ovaries, 140
Ovaries and testes, " stones," 121, 122
Oval stones as life emblems in graves, 140

P

Pal, 84
Pala, religious name, 64
Pala, pale, pestle, or phallus was piercer, 88-89
Pala, Phala, Phallis, Phallus, Phallos, 63
Pharoah should be Phalao or Pala-O, 63
Phal to phil, 200 philos, 89, 90
Pall, Palladium, palas, etc., 141, 142
Palace from pala, 141
Pala, series of stones, paling, 142
Pala cross, Tsur (Colenso), 75
Palaki, Indian sacred prostitutes, 105
Pala gave rise to palace, etc., 84
Pal, Tsur, El, root words, phallic, in Aramaic, etc., 81-83
Pala a god, so " God is love " correct, 89
Palladium, phallus, god, 141, 142, 143
Pala, sexual, phallus, etc., 10, 11
Pal, phallus, derivatives, 81
Pal, tsur, and el, a world of men, places, and things produced, 81

Pala, male organ, 61, 62, 63
Pala, Hindoo for male organ, corrupted, all vowels used, 61-62
Pala, written pela, phallus, pal, phil, phyl, pole, pale, pel, phalas, phara, etc., 61, 62
Pala derivatives, 141, 143
Pala source of names in hundreds 75, 76
Pala, phallus, phil, phyl, Greeks, 62, 142
Pala in hieroglyphics, Budge's text book, 64
Pala, upright thing, the pala or phallus, male organ, 70
Pale, pile, pole, etc., Tsur, rock, cross, rod of god or Midian middle part, Maté, Moses' rod, Matthew, 85
Pala in place names, 83, 84
Pala, pole, etc., pul, 89
Pala, many derivatives, 84-85
Pala, words derived from, 141, 142
Pala or pole, root of metropolis, acropolis, etc., 100
Pala, pillar, post, 141, 142
Pala in English words, 141
Palas, goddess of knowledge, (and Adam knew his wife), 142
Phallic pillars, 400 in Cornwall alone (Schliemann, Troy), thousands of small models at all temples dredged up from rivers show circumcision marks in all religions, cross, 72, 73
Palaki, female of pala, Indian prostitutes (sacred), 105
Palas in page of hieroglyphics, Budge, Palla in hieroglyphics, 64
Palestine always held by Egypt, see explorers from Philadelphia University, 86

" Palestine " unknown till created by Romans, 20, 21

Palestine, Philistine, etc., 84

Palestine, only Egyptian buildings, 15

Palestine always under Egypt, 16, 17

Palestine Egyptian, then Roman, 87, 88

" Palestine " a name applicable even to England ; all were phallic worshippers, 90

Palestine held by Egypt, 15, 16

Palestine name created 700 A.D., no such land held by Egypt, Beisan, 85, 86

Palestine, land of the pala, 16, 17

Palestine unknown till Romans created the word, 17

Palestine unknown (by name), 85

Palestine always under Egypt, 20, 21

Palestine and Philistine the same, 17

Palestine and Philistine same words created by the Romans, 17

Palestine always held by Egypt, 20, 21

Palestine pathway between Egypt and Babylon, etc., 19

Palestine Roman through Egypt conquest, 16

Palestine held by Egypt for hundreds of years B.C., 20, 21

Pall over dead, 141

Papa for Pope, god on earth, 31

Paraphernalia, 68

Paraphernalia should be Palaphernalia, all church utensils, etc., phallic, hence pala, 68

Patriarchs invented, 83

Patriatchs mythical (Encyc. Bib.), 27

Paul visited great centres of prostitution, 59–60

Paul's visits to centres of prostitution, 59 60

Paul's visits to towns of filthy sensuality, 58

Paul's voyages apocryphal, 83

Paul a myth, 58–59

Paul a pen-creation by priests, 58, 59

Paul a myth (Encyc. Bib.), 58, 59

Paul creation of priestly pen, 59

Paul created to argue the " uncircumcision," 59, 60

Paul is simply pala, the male organ, pawl, pall from pala, 60

Paul visited places of filthy sensuality. Deification of lust (Encyc. Bib.). Early Christians lay all night in the temple, 56

Paul visits all great centres of prostitution, Antioch, Lystra, Salamis, Papho, Perga, Pisidia, Pamphilia, Iconium, Athens and Corinth, 59–60

Paul is pala, phala, pale, pole, the phallus or male organ, 60

Paul's cities famed for filthy sensuality, 110

Paul's Epistles to unify the Hebrew and European religions as to circumcision, 58–59

Paul is said to have visited towns which were hot-beds of prostitution, 58 et seq.

Encyc. Bib. says, " Irrevocably passed away " (article Paul), no Epistle of Paul, verdict of the Encyc. Bib. authority, 59

Payne Knight's Worship of Priapus, pornographic illustrations of Roman sculpture, 34

Pebbles in graves, 2 little quartz stones as testicles, 140

Peel towers, 115–116

Peel tower, pala, Haig, Scotland, 115–116

Penalties (death) for touching holy things, 7–8

Penalties (death) for pronouncing holy name, 7–8

People beginning to understand phallism, 8

Persians (no Hebrew in Palestine), 132, 133

Persian religion, 70

Persian legend of creation, 11

P-Es-El, Idol, Mesek, I-d-ol, pillar god, 48

Pesel, pestle, phallus, piercer, 88

Pesel, 88

Pestilence, evil condition of the pessel, or pestle, male organ, 70

Pesel, 47

Peter (old cult), circumcision, 60

Peter and Paul, Petros and Pala, 187

" Phallic " means sexual, 11

Phalli everywhere, 90

Phalli dredged up from the Tiber, Seine and Thames Rivers, 48

Phallos (Greek), and phallus (Roman), 63–64

Phallus and Phallos, 63

Phalli worshipped from China to Peru, 90

Phallic emblem in Italy, hung on wrist, Sir W. Hamilton, 38

Phallic words disguised, 48–50

Phallus from pala, Hindoo, 11

Phallus + oil = " living god," 91

Phallic feasts in Rome and India, 38, 44

Phallic origin of Bible names, 110, 111

Phallic pillars, lost pyx, pixie, 122

Phalla O, Pala O, Phara O, 114, 115

Phallic words and sacred things, 141

Phallic leaping and playing, 134

Phallic god, Behemoth, 133

Phallic in Bible literature, 135

Phara-O, Pharoah, 115

Phalakra, plus ankh, double-sex, 100

Phara-oh, not Fairo, 114

Phallic Hebrew words and practices, 80

Phara-oh, corrupted in English to Fair-oh, 63

Phallic cult natural to Rome, 33

Phallic origin of sacred things, 9–11

Phallic cult adopted by Rome, 33

Phalakra, " bald-headed," but really point of phallus, very bald, 100

Phallic models, 37, 38

Phala, Pharaoh, 37

Pharaoh is Pala-oh, male and female—a god, 63

Pharaoh, Pala O, Osar, 114, 115

Pharaoh not " Fair-oh " but Fara-oh, 65

Pharaoh mispronounced, 114

Phallic words vulgar, 8, 9

Phallic words double-sexed, 8

Phallic symbols base of religion 7

Pharaoh should be Phala-O, 62–63

Philadelphia University, discoveries in Palestine, 17

50,000 Philistines died through touching the Hebrew ark, woman, 49, 50

Philistines, a name made by Romans, 16–17

Philistine, land of love, or the phallus, or merely prostitution of Philises, 17

Philistine created by Romans, 16, 17

Phillis changed to almond, woman, 92

Pillars, crosses, and phalli in thousands round ancient temples, 72, 73, 74

Piercer, 70, 88

Pillar god, 48

Pillar-letter "I" abolished, represented by a comma, 14

Pillars and crosses, world-wide, 74, 75

Pillar-letter "I," 9, 14

Pillar and cross the same, 76–77

Pixie, pyx, cross, 122

Pixie, pyx, 122

Pope's mandate sudden, complete and implacable, 31

Political use of priests, 4

Pornographic images, gods, and idols, 38–39

Pornographic Romans, 80, 81

Pornographic images found in Tiber, Seine and Thames on dredging, 47, 48

Power of priests' frightfulness, 119

Priests' commercial exploitation of prostitution, 42

Polytheistic Bible-god Elohim, 10

Processions of arks in Egypt, 166–167

Prostitutes at temples, records of 1,000, 103–104

Priapic Romans wrote the Bible, 80–81

Priests keep concubines, some too poor, 44, 45

Priapic orgies in Rome in presence of women and children, 80, 81

Priests brothel keepers, 14, 15

Priests keepers of holy women for prostitution, 125

Priests and people naked, so no shame, 61

Priests took fees (white slaves), 105

Priests dancing with naked palals, 57

Protestants' false "Word of God," 18

Prostitutes attached to all temples, 105, 106

Prostitutes sought in marriage, 106

Prostitutes, sacred, terrible fate of, 108, 110

Prostitutes placed above "honest women," 57, 58

Prostitution hire, temple treasury, 108, 109

Protestants wished to use Roman symbols, but disguise by the use of J for I, Jew for IU, 18, 19

Protestants' dishonesty, 19

Protestants "blasphemy," 18–19

Pseudepigrapha, "sham writings," Bible composed of (Encyc. Bib.), 110

"Ptolemy" a title, 2, 3

Ptolemy Soter 300 B.C., but no such name as Palestine known, 151

Ptolemy Soter, Ptah-mes Soter, 2

Pyx, a rod, like Moses's Maté, 122

Ptah-mes Soter, Son of God, the Saviour, 2

Ptolemy Soter's ideas of government, 2, 3

Ptolemy Soter, universal religion for ruling, 23

Ptolemies not blood relations, 3

Ptolemy XIV, 3

Ptolemy III, 3

Ptolemy Soter, "Ptah-mes Soter, Son of God the Saviour," 3

Ptolemy Soter started new movement for universal religion, 3

Ptolemy a title, not a family name, 3

Ptolemy's collection of Scriptures, 3

Ptolomæus a title, not a name, 3

Pulpit, double-sex, two sex organs, 161

Pulpit, pul the phallus, pit the yoni, double-sexed, 137

Purim and Kipurim, 98

Phallic emblems on children's wrists, etc., 38

Palestine, name unknown till Romans coined the same, 15–16

Pulpit, "high place"; pulpit is born or high place, Bamoth plural is brothel, 137, 161

R

Rachel stole her father's Seraphim, 124–125

R and L interchangeable, 97, 114

Religions all phallic, 69–70

Religious prostitution beyond dawn of history, 60

Religious prostitution, terrible cruelty, 108, 109

Rebekah, mother of thousands of millions, 23

Religious documents collected at Alexandria, 2

"Red thing" widely applied, 35, 36

Rod of god and two stones, male organ, 77–78

Rod and almond, male and female, 105, 106

Rod of god, stones, and ark = creative god, 76

R and L interchangeable, some nations one letter, and pal changed, 97

Rome's oath on Bible, 32

Romans acquired Palestine when they conquered Egypt, 20, 21

Rome's Catholic religion, 33, 34

Rome combines all religions, 198, 199

Rome could not hold all her conquests, 23

Rome's failure to hold conquests by sword, 29–30

Rome's conquests necessitated a universal religion, 193, 194

Romans invented Hebrew, 25, 26

Rome's college of priests to create Bible, 31, 32

Rome creates new alphabet on which to found religion and god names, 8, 9

Romans invented Hebrew as sacred script to found the Bible, 86–87

Rome conceived Bible as a cement of her ragged Empire, 153

Roman creation of a "Church," 19, 20

Rome created a power above kings, 153

Rome created religion for government, 23

Rome to control through priests, with rack, stake, and confessional, 31

Rome's ban terrible, 30, 31

Rod of god, 2 stones in ark, 122

Rod of god and 2 stones in the ark, 116

Rod and almond (Magdalen), 200

Rod of god and 2 stones, 85

Rod from Midian, 85

Rod and almond, 127

Rock that begat thee, Tsur, 70

Rod and almond, 92, 93

Rod of god in Midian (middle part), 85

Rome's curse paralysing, 30, 31

Rome conceived "universal religion," to bind her conquests, 23

Rome's curse feared, 153, 154

Rome's new sacred alphabet, Hebrew, 14

Rome's difficulty in keeping Europe, conceived cement of universal religion, 153, 154

Rome and India, phallic feasts, 38–43

Rome's religious conspiracy for enslavement of mankind, 194–195

Rome's universal religion, Catholic, 1

Rome's scheme for universal dominion, 29, 30, 31

Rome's scheme of priest control, 1, 2

Rome slaughtered priests of other religions, 195

Rome's false history, 21, 22

Romans composed Bible to enslave mankind, 185

Rome's secret organisation, 154

Rome's ecclesiastics at every court, 30, 31

Rome ruled through ecclesiastics, 31

Rome's universal religion and book, 31

Rome's Empire to be saved by religion, 1

Roman fêtes highly phallic. Outrageous songs, children joining in, Cato, 38, 39

Roman fête days, 12 per year, 38

Roman pornography, 35, 37

Romans gave Christna, Hindoo god, first place, 23

Rome creates Bible, 31, 32

Roman destruction and construction, 28, 29

Rome hopes to rule through priests, 23

Rome, centre of grossest pornography, 33

Rome's sex orgies, 33

Romans create " Hebrew " to disguise phallic meaning of letters, 132

Rome very phallic and produced a phallic Bible, 141

Rome's combined religion, 1

Roman symbolism (detail), 129 132

Rome's revelation to men, 1

Rome built the Bible new language in life creators, 127

Rome's search for scriptures of Europe, Egypt, Western Asia India, 1, 2

Rome's Son of God, 22

Rome's Empire crumbling, 1

Romans made new language, 24

Rome's 12 priapic feasts, 15

Rome's infernal means of government, 31, 39

Rome's sacred signs or symbols, 33

Rome decides to control through religion, 107

Roman letters too obvious, hence creation of Hebrew, 14

Rome created Hebrew and Jews, 32–33

Roman illegitimacy, 43, 44

Roman colony at Galilee, 1, 4

Roman college to evolve new religion, 4

Roman Catholics debased, 185

Rome's universal religion, 196

Rome extremely licentious. 38, 39

Rome's Catholic Bible, 33

Rome's powerful engine of government, rack and confessional, 31

Romans' Hebrew composed by theory, could not be pronounced nor spoken, 24, 25

Romans created Philistines, 16

Rome unable to crush revolts, 2

Rome hoped to consolidate her Empire, 2

Rome introduced serpent worship, 107–108

Rome's naked orgies in full daylight, 38-39
Rome called male organ phallus, 64-65
Rome's reason for "universal religion," 23
Romans separated their religion from all Zodiacal signs, 209, 210
Rome could conquer in detail, 107
Rome's Empire too large for sword control, 2
Rome adopted phallic cult, 33
R and L, T and D, each replace the other, 36-37
Rome's creation of Bible, 31, 32
Rome's creation of secret language, 32, 33
Bible which could be read by the people not safe, so Rome creates "Hebrew" Bible, 31, 32
Romans invented new alphabet and language and called it Hebrew, 9, 32, 33
Romans acquired Palestine on conquering Egypt, 20, 21
Romans decided to alter letters which expressed sex, I, O, U, and V, 127-132

S

S, feminine, 145
St. Augustine, clean linen, as the "holy kiss" was administered, 44, 106
St. Augustine, Eucharist sexual, 106
Sacred letters disguised, 14
St. Mary of the Ovaries, Southwark Cathedral, 140
St. Mary of Ovaries, 121
St. Augustine on "holy kiss," 44
Sacred serpent was the cobra, 124

Sacred cobra, Indian sign, 124
Sacred prostitutes (general notes) 108 (Encyc. Bib.)
Sacred things, holy secret, 10, 11
Sacred member 12, 6
Sacred names founded on a few letters, 119
Samples of author's notes (Appendix)
Sarah, Terah, form Seraphim, and Teraphim, serpent idols, 124, 125
Sarah's name means a god (Encyc. Bib., 4,284), 113
Sarah, Terah, Seraphim, Teraphim, 113
Sarah (Encyc. Bib.), 112
Sarah, god, double-sex, 113
Sarah and Terah, 113, 114
Saviours all crossed, 146
Saviour Soter, common word, 144
Saviours were all suns, 146
Saviour common title, 144
Secret signs for sex words, 12, 13, 14
Secret methods of church control, 31
Selaoth or Lesakoth, 46
Semen, seed, Latin in Hebrew, 77
"Seph," serpent, universal symbol of the male organ, 11
Serapeum Library called after Serapis, Egyptian god, 3
Serapeum Library saved, 3
Seraphim, 113, 114, 124
Seraphim and Teraphim, 113, 114, 124
Seraphim, Teraphim, 124
Serapeum Library preserved, 3
Seraphim brazen serpents, 124, 125
Serpent, cobra, 124
Serpent religion, 124
Serpent symbol everywhere, 124

Serpent ubiquitous in religion, 124

Serpent more subtle should be more naked, 143

Serpent symbol used all over the world, 11

Serpent most worshipped symbol of deity, yet it was the "phallus," and never mentioned as such in *Encys. Bib.*, 123-125

Serpent sexual passion, Joseph, IOseph, man and woman, with serpent, sexual passion, 113-114

Story of Eden, 114

Servitude is the badge of all our race here, 21-22

Several centuries to produce Bible, 3-4

Sexual god dangerous to Church, 111

Sexual intercourse a confession of faith, 105

Sex orgies universal, 47-50

Sex words have secret signs, 7, 8, 9

Sex names for gods vulgar, 8

Sham writings, pseudepigrapha (*Encys. Bib.* so describes the Bible), 79, 110

Siddarth's teaching copied by Romans as that of Jesus, 192, 193

Siddartha, 195, 196

Sin, "deadly," is doubt, 185

Sir William Hamilton, phallic models, 38

Sul, origin of Tsur, 77

Slaves for prostitution in Egypt, 60

Sodomy practised by "consecrated" men, 106

Soldier executed for touching the monstrance and pyx, 122

Solar religion based on 12 months and signs of the Zodiac, 5-6

Solar symbolism number, 7, 12

Solomon a myth, 152

Solomon unknown, 20

Solomon a fictitious character, 20

Solomon, thousand millions of bullion, 22-23

Solomon (invented), 20

Solomon's glory all a myth, Colenso, 87

Solomon, 5,000 tons gold, and 50,000 tons silver, 20, 22

Solomon, "banner," 125

Solomon, thousand million, 23

Some of these personages had no existence. If some, why not all? Who is to discriminate? 110

Southwark Cathedral, ovaries, 140

Staff for O, U, V, 14

Stone altars still flow with oil, 77, 78

Stones wrapped together with strength, 136

"Stones," secret spring of breath of life, H, 120

Stones (testes) in graves of Oban, 140

"Stones," testes, and ovaries, H, 120-121

Stones, 8, 9, 140

Struggle for existence kills kindness, 193

Sun-worship, 180, 181

Sun, the saviour, 212

Sun mechanical, not a god, 184

Sun not "free-willed," 184

Sun god in Bible, 158

Son of god, Saviour, Iesu and Ptolemy, 2-3

Sur, Sul, 112

"Sul" in names, 115

Susannah, 34

Symbolical letters, 1

Symbolical writing, 14

Syphilis, Palestine, Philistine, 89, 90

Syphilis incurable, 201

"Syrian Goddess," of Lucian, 44

T

Tabernacle, Dolphins' skins, womb, 123

Tabernacle, Dolphins' skins, delphis, womb, 123

Tamar and Judah, 45

Temple or church income entirely from prostitution, 57

Temple harlots trained to the duties all over the world, "serpent worship," prostitution, 108, 109

Temples were brothels, 45, 46

Temple women Magdalenes, 92, 93

Temple women Kadeshoth, nuns, pisces, fishes, 93

The Encyc. Bib. says a special class of temple harlot was maintained. The hire was brought into the treasury (brothel keeping), 55–56

Tetragrammaton, death to speak of or pronounce IHOH, 141

Tetragrammaton unpronounceable, 7–8

Tetragrammaton, holy IHOH, 7

Testes symbolised by H, breath of life, 120

Testes sacred, curse on those without testes, 120

Testimonies and ovaries, 140

Twelve texts, "God in the flesh," for Jesus, 156, 157, 168

Thousand prostitutes at one temple, 43

Terrible diseases from religious prostitution, 200–201

Teraphim, 114

Terah a god, 112

Testes and ovaries, 120

Ti, Di, Chinese, 8

Timgad, 28, 29

Titus, great gifts at Paphos, Cyprus, 45

Three-letter named god, Eli, 10

Thor's "hammer" phallic, 116

Thor's hammer, Minoan double-axe, 116

Three-in-one, 122

The most holy combination did not last very long, totally abandoned (ark), 139

Town names phallic, list, 97

Tilling the ground, 35

Tsur, a source of names, 75, 112

Trisul, 76

Tower, Tzur, rock, 95

Tyberya is Galilee, 196

Tyberya Lake re-named by Romans Galilee, 5

Tor's hammer, 116

Tower is Tur, from Tzur, "Rock that begat thee," 95

Tsur, 112–115

Tsur, root of Bible names (list), 75, 81, 102

Tsur, "Rock that begat thee" derivative, 81, 83

Tsur, "Rock that begat thee," 70

Tsur, "Rock that begat thee," 77

Tsur, root word in many languages, 101

Tsur split into Tur and Sur, 101–102

Tsur, derivative Sar, Tar, etc., 102

Tsur, root of many names, 81

Tur and Sur with other vowels make names, 81

True basis of hundreds of names, 76

True meaning of names fatal to Bible, 5

Twelve a symbolic number, 7

Twelve everywhere in Bible, 7

Two sex-gods= everlasting life, 111

Twelve in religion, 7

Twelve naked orgies, in Rome per year, 15

Tsur, root of bi-sexual names, 112, 113

Two sexes symbolical of eternal life, 5

U

Uapés, on the Amazon, worship of Jurapari, 41

Umma, 130

Una, similar to IUNO or Juno, 130

U and V replace O, 9

Unable to hold Empire by the sword, Rome got up a Bible, 152

Universal religion, 2

Universal religion to end war, 2

Universal religion to save Roman Empire, 1

Uzza struck dead, touching Ark, 139

V

Vowels of Hebrew, 123

Virgin worship, Jacob, 54

Virgo intacta worship, 54

Virgo (ladder to heaven), 54

W

Word made Flesh, 198

Word Jew, a fraud, 18

Words from pala, 83–91

Women as the keystone of Church doors, 34

Writers of Bible form a phallic nation, 5

Writers of Bible criticism declare Hebrews were never a nation, 87

Writers of Bible say Hebrews lived under other tribes, 87

What sort of a god do we worship? 111, 112

Y

Yogis naked (holy), 61

Yima, Persian creator, 11

Yaisu Kreestos, Jesus Christ, 146

"Yaisu" the pronunciation of Jesus, 24

Yima creates life by ring and dagger, 70

Yima, dagger and ring to create life, 11

Young maidens go up hill to fetch water (Jack and Jill), 137

Yogis in India go quite naked, 61

Z

Zend of Persia, 132

CPSIA information can be obtained at www.ICGtesting.com
Printed in the USA
LVOW071929240612

287426LV00013B/166/A